IT'S ALL IN THE FACE

The Key to Finding
Your Life Purpose

Naomi R. Tickle

Daniel's Publishing, Mountain View, California

IT'S ALL IN THE FACE

The Key to Finding Your Life Purpose

Naomi R. Tickle

Published by: Daniel's Publishing
Post Office Box 4439
Mountain View, California 94040, USA

Copyright C 1997 by Naomi R. Tickle
First Printing 1995
Library of Congress Catalog Card Number 97-66570

ISBN 0-9646-3981-5

Printed in the United States
10 9 8 7 6 5 4 3 2 1

Photographs of Celebrities by Shooting Stars International
Art work by Edward Fowler
Book cover illustration by Tana Powell, San Francisco
Book cover design by Karen Monroe of Monroe Graphics
Inside illustrations by Alex Mauser

ACKNOWLEDGMENTS

This book would not have been possible without the opportunity to meet and study with some of the people responsible for the development of Personology. Robert Whiteside, pioneer and founder of Personology, and William Burtis who, along with several other dedicated personologists, were responsible for the science known today as Personology. The late Suzanne Caygill (founder of color analysis in 1945), whose work inspired me to seek further a greater understanding of the patterns and designs seen in the human being. To my husband Andrew for his incredible patience and support for my work over the past 15 years. To my friends Cindi Lynch, Lorraine Kamisky and George Roman whose contributions and continued support have been greatly appreciated. Thanks are due to Bruce Vaughan for his insight on jury selection, and to Don Wilson (who has used personology for over forty years) for his encouragement and enthusiasm. My thanks go to Jim Pendleberry and other fellow personologists who have devoted many years to the development and promotion of personology. To my clients for their support and inspiration, and to the many people who have shared their success stories with me regarding the impact that Personology has had on their lives.

FOREWORD

Personology relates the human physical structure to the native behavioral functioning process. The premise and major theme of personology is that structure pre-disposes or inclines function, but *freedom of choice* can overcome structure. Over the years, growing attention has been focused on the relationship between physical structure in humans and their behavior. There is now known to be a correlation between personology and the basic sciences of physiology, anatomy and neurology. The science of genetics also plays a role in the study of personological factors and traits.

Today, teachers and counselors in the field of personology are able to provide their students and clientele with specific, down-to-earth information and recommendations on better understanding of their own make-up, relating more effectively to family members, improving human relations on the job or in the political arena and selecting the right career.

Personology helps people to take a more practical approach to all aspects of daily living.

William F. Burtis, M.S. Personologist

TABLE OF CONTENTS

1. Let's Face It   1

2. Historical Background   3

3. Concepts   7

4. Physical Traits   17

5. Automatic Expression   41

6. Feelings and Emotions   73

7. Thinking Traits   115

8. Famous Faces   132

9. Traits In Action   143

10. Application To Life's Daily Experience   157

11. The Key to Finding Your Life Purpose   169

12. Creating a Map for Your Life   175

13. Self Assesment Test   175

14 Glossary of Terms   189

15. Index   193

16. Appendix   196

*We meet ourselves time and again
in a thousand disguises on the paths of life.*

-Carl Jung

LET'S FACE IT

We all read faces, we can't avoid it. It's both an ancient art and a modern science. Some get more useful information from it than others. In the pace of business activities and personal life, we are constantly meeting new people and reaffirming our relationships and expectations of those familiar to us. There is seldom time to get to know and understand individuals before important decisions and agreements are made.

It is always easier to deal with people and faces we know. This is why in business we generally keep the same suppliers and customers. We also tend to keep the same friends, doctors, dentists, plumbers and family photographers.

Today, many corporations recognize their employee's needs to understand each other better before they can work together effectively. To this end they have used written tests to categorize psychological and personality traits. Workshops have also been used successfully. Groups study each other's behavior and label it as the majority perceives it. Some participants use small place cards on their desks to announce their personal styles as *expressive amiable, analytical driver, etc.* This may seem extreme to anyone who has not been involved in the process. However, it does show the importance people quickly attach to each other before working together. This is fine for corporations, however, the rest of us need something which gives similar results without written tests or lengthy behavior study. Many professions now recognize that face reading can provide critical information quickly.

Commonly used expressions such as *a nose for news, highbrow, tight lip* and *conehead* show that we associate facial features with behavior. Cartoonists and casting directors for film and theater strive to select faces that convince us of the characters portrayed. The relationship of facial structure to the personality within has intrigued and puzzled scientists since early times. The serious study of faces, and their relationship to the personality within, originated independently in China, ancient Greece with Pythagoras (of triangle fame) and Aristotle. In the Roman Empire it became a respected profession. In England, during the reign of Elizabeth the First, it was considered a threat to the authorities and was punishable by whipping. In the twentieth century three men changed it into a modern science, Edward Vincent Jones, Robert Whiteside and William Burtis.

Edward Vincent Jones, was a California judge, who categorically linked facial features and character traits. Robert Whiteside worked on statistically validating these linkages, and was subsequently joined by William Burtis. They continued the testing and correlation of over seventy facial features and behavior traits.

In activities as diverse as jury selection, selling face to face, and resolving family problems, faces are spelling out vital information. This book is an illustrated guide designed to help you recognize facial features that indicate how people will react.

HISTORICAL BACKGROUND
OF PERSONOLOGY

When early man gazed on the ferocious face of the crocodile he must have been struck by the relationship between appearance and behavior. We might have expected this to be extended, in a more detailed and subtle way, to the study of his fellow men. We might expect that this study would have developed into a science of it's own, at least as old as the written word itself. In fact this did not happen until the twentieth century.

Why so many centuries of delay?

One investigator of appearance and behavior, in the sixth century B.C., was the Greek philosopher Pythagoras. His concern was the "soul" of man. Today we have to recognize that was a far tougher project than his geometry theorems. Two centuries later, in the fourth century B.C., Aristotle came up with the intriguing notion of understanding man's character by comparing his qualities and appearance with similar qualities and appearances in animals. Eventually the interest in Greece and Europe moved toward the practical understanding of people.

As time passed, through the Dark Ages and the Middle Ages, interest in the appearance-behavior concept came and went. It was tied in with astrological divination's and then forgotten, and never established on its own. We have to remember in those days things were very different from today.

In those far off days there was not a scientific method, nor a scientific culture as we know it today. It was more of a mind game. The philosophers dealt much more in ideas (theory) than they did in

3

actual information (data). If an idea was sufficiently brilliant or appealing it might be accepted without today's burden of proof. However if attempts were made to put the scheme to serious use before proper (modern) testing, then results could be unpredictable. There was often a real barrier to new knowledge and ideas, however important, when they contradicted or competed with established doctrines and politics. Remember the opposition to abandoning the flat earth in favor of the round one, and having the planets orbit the sun instead of the earth? Then there was the case of a man arrested for fraud, when he claimed he could transmit voice by wire.

So without the scientific muscle and will, it is not surprising that any use was made of the appearance-behavior concept until the present century. The old world simply was not ready for it.

What emerged throughout Europe during the Age of Enlightenment, and into the early part of the nineteenth century, was a common theory that certain human body shapes had an effect on human behavior. A trio of German doctors - Lavater, Gall and Spurzheim - developed a comprehensive thesis based on this supposition.

From these well known scientists work a surge of popularity was spawned for phrenology (the study of the shape of the human skull and its relationship to human personality) throughout Germany, Austria and France at the turn of the twentieth century. Even the European medical community seriously explored phrenology and conducted extensive research into the relationship between phrenology, biochemistry, and the genetic make up of an individual.

It was during this time that the American George Fowler brought these studies and the various findings on phrenology to the United States. He became a noted phrenologist in his own right, as well as a New York society darling until he and his work fell into disrepute.

4

While phrenology was gaining popular attention in Europe and Fowler was enjoying success in the U.S., the philosopher Hans Christian Smutz emerged as Prime Minister of South Africa. His compelling interest into the relationship between ethnic and genetic origins led him to coin the term personology.

It was Edward Vincent Jones, a California judge, who put the subject on modern footing. He wanted to know if certain behavior traits correlated with physical features.

Judge Jones had many opportunities to study the physical features and the behavior of defendants, witnesses and attorneys for the prosecution and the defense. He recorded facial features and the characteristics that accompanied them. As the amount of data accumulated Jones saw that there were clear-cut trends. He devoted his time to research much of what had already been established and extracted from these studies the traits that were consistent. He was the first person to take these established observations and put them into a usable form. He termed it personology - literally the study of persons. Years later he met Robert Whiteside, whose interest matched his own intensity for the subject.

Robert Whiteside continued the research and supplied the statistical testing and validation. The system was further developed to use detailed measurements of over one hundred traits.

When a man does not know what harbor he is making for,
no wind is the right wind.

-Seneca

CONCEPTS

Faces and Behavior

The behavior traits described in this book, and the facial features that predict them, were discovered purely by repeated observation by Edward Vincent Jones during thousands of courtroom cases. Robert Whiteside [Reference 1] later validated these findings along with William Burtis. In 1950 Robert Whiteside directed a study of 1,050 adults from California and Oregon. Measurements of sixty-eight facial features were recorded and correlated with personality factors using standard statistical techniques. In order to determine where these traits were located, they divided the head into five areas. The thinking traits are in the frontal area, feelings and emotions in the eye area, the expression traits from under the eye to the base of the chin and the action traits are located in the top portion of the head. The analysis of the results showed an impressive 92% accuracy-per-trait.

A later survey of 492 individuals showed that vocational recommendations based on facial analysis were 92% accurate based on self professed job satisfaction. When personology information was used in marriage, couples were helped in 88% of the cases.

In 1943 a study was conducted with the freshmen Air Force class to determine the career path for each student. The information later was found to be 97% accurate. In 1963 additional studies, headed up by Robert Whiteside, were also made at San Quinton prison. The purpose of this study was to find if there was a relationship between the crime committed and the face structure. The study did show relationship correlation. However, this does not mean to say that every person with those particular traits is automatically a criminal. Choice always supersedes structure.

7

Face reading is based on facts. Although some publishers and bookstores place it in the supernatural category, it has no relation to mysticism, spirituality or altered states of consciousness. However, people skilled in these areas will appreciate the insights which can be gained from reading faces.

Since there is no underlying theory or explanation to grasp, face reading is a very simple and uncomplicated exercise. What you see is what you get!

Disclaimers

In the past, reading faces has been associated with fields as widely divergent as astrology and structural genetics. It is important here to state some disclaimers.

Face reading, as described in this book, is not involved with genetics since we are not concerned with characteristics of the parents, only the individual. Neither are we concerned how a trait was inherited (i.e., from the mother's or father's side of the family), nor are we concerned with which genes control it.

The innate abilities and characteristics we inherit are only one of the forces controlling our lives. Early nurturing and the experiences of childhood (and later) strongly shape the growth of our personalities. Of course, after childhood we can still, by conscious desire and choice, change our attitudes, behavior and activities.

We assert only that we are born with certain easily recognizable features in the face which become clearly discernible during childhood and then remain for life; and that these features accurately predict behavior and personality traits.

Enhancing Your Perception

Whenever we see a new face, we are instinctively aware of the gender and age, which we record with no conscious effort. The facial features spell out information on character traits that we can learn to read and interpret as automatically as we read gender and age. Within the first thirty seconds of interacting with a new person we form opinions. Are they friendly, quiet, aloof, casual, formal, trustworthy or confident? Do they look successful or do they look tough and hardened by life's experiences? We might make a comment that the individual looks as if they've had a tough day at work. We form these opinions based on observable facial expressions and structure. As we learn to recognize new facial features, and become confident of the traits they predict it becomes a part of our immediate perception. With these skills we already know many things about new individuals before a single word has been spoken.

Trait Combinations

A behavior trait on its own may not be that significant, particularly if it is not a strong one. However if this trait occurs in combination with other traits, the effect may be strongly modified or reinforced. For example, if an individual is extremely aggressive and forceful these traits may be moderated by their sensitivity and considerateness.

Asymmetrical Faces - Mood swings

The stronger the differences between the two sides of the face, the greater are the mood swings. This is the result of the parents being significantly different from each other in their appearance. The child inherits physical features from each parent, the right side reflects the father's traits and the left side the mother's. Some people may feel they have dual personalities because of the push and pull of the different traits. For example, one moment a person may be very tolerant and the next very intolerant, sometimes they are very competitive and other times it does not concern them. The person has no idea when their mood will change, it may happen within five minutes. They can be on cloud nine in one moment and then suddenly the whole world is on their shoulders and/or they become very depressed. These mood changes are as puzzling to the individual as they are to others. They appear to be very inconsistent and unpredictable. Too much caffeine or other drugs may add to the mood shift. However, this may happen without any outside influences. Once the person has a personology profile and the traits have been identified by a personologist, they have a better grasp of what is occuring. Consequently, they have better control over their own life.

There are several approaches to managing these moods. Some people find meditation significantly helps to balance them. Others find exercising or engaging in an activity helps to change the inner conversation. The solution is to recognize when the mood changes occur. If the mood change is negative take immediate action. Do not make important decisions when you are on the down side of your mood and be alert to situations that trigger the moods.

Establish goals that will keep you on tract. This is important, particularly if you are starting a business. This is a time when you experience yourself going through peaks and valleys, which is typical of a new business.

On the positive side, people who score high on mood swings have a broader range of interests and are very versatile. They may go through several successful career changes in their life time.

Instinctive Behavior and Learned Behavior
The fact that a person has low innate self-confidence does not imply a value judgment, nor does it imply a difficulty coping with life. First let's look at how we understand the word *self-confidence*. We all agree that it is good to have self-confidence. We like to have it in ourselves and to see it in others. It gives us

the reassuring feeling that people know what they are doing. Self-confidence may be innate (inherited) or learned. The way people handle new situations is revealing about self-confidence. An innately self-confident person will welcome new situations and will handle any problem that occurs on the fly. People with lower self-confidence do not look forward to surprises and experience an inner turmoil when not familiar with the task at hand. This is especially so when asked to suddenly give a presentation to an audience. They like to be well informed ahead of time and will not take on a task unless they are very familiar with the information ahead of time. This thorough preparation can make them successful and thus becomes a learned behavioral pattern. People with innately high or innately low self-confidence will both be successful, but use different approaches.

Conscious Choice

Although we have inherited traits, which stay with us for life, we do have control over our behavior and the way in which those traits are expressed. Once our traits are identified we can consciously choose to suppress a basic urge when it is not appropriate. Take for example someone who has a high temper, is extremely physical, forceful and ruthless. This person might be inclined towards violence. However, once the individual is aware of his/her innate characteristics, he/she can choose to gain control of these traits and use their energy in a more productive and supportive way. In fact, these types of people can learn to avoid or remove themselves from situations which stimulate negative actions. Another example would be someone who is always late for appointments. This would indicate high tolerance. People with this trait can discipline themselves to arrive on time once they know this is part of their inherent nature. The choice is ultimately each individual's decision and responsibility.

Our Mixed Heritage

The different species of birds build their nests with distinct shapes. The robin, swallow and eagle will each stay with their own unchanging style of nest year after year, and generation after generation. The fixed patterns and preferred environments are so important that migratory birds travel thousands of miles to nest in a specific place. When the human race spread throughout the world it adapted, like the wild life, to each region and its environment. However, unlike wildlife, there are now very few regions of the earth where racial "purity" still exists, since racial characteristics are no longer vital to surviving the local conditions. Mankind has now emerged with complex patterns resulting from its mixed heritage.

Today, humans live in surroundings that may be quite different from their inherited mixtures of natural habitats and environmental preferences. When our lifestyle includes activities, in our career or hobbies, that bring us a deep level of satisfaction our attention focuses more easily and naturally on what we are doing. Think of the times when you have engaged in activities which have really brought enjoyment. How did you feel at that time? Did you experience a deep sense of satisfaction? These moments are some of the key indicators in finding your Life Purpose.

By understanding and identifying our innate patterns, there is a strong sense of self-validation. There is also a feeling of being more centered, and less influenced by commercial pressures which tell us what we should buy and how we should spend our time.

There is a resonance that we feel, when surrounded by the colors, designs and environment we enjoy. We feel "in tune" with our lives, with a piece of music we listen to, being by the water or walking through the woods, playing tennis or shooting the rapids.

Self-Knowledge

The quest for Self-Knowledge, which was once regarded as fanciful introspection, has progressed to bookshelves dedicated to self-understanding, self-awareness, self-discipline, self-education, self-improvement, etc. The ideas expounded vary greatly on each author's view about what you are born with, what you grew up with and what to do about it. Face reading provides a good starting point for understanding what traits we inherited at birth. In short, understanding personality traits is useful to anyone who deals with other people (and who doesn't?). But despite the many practical business applications of personology, this book is also intended for the individual to use as a practical guide in everyday life. Understanding your own traits is a critical first step towards becoming the individual you want to be.

This book does not claim that personology performs miracles, nor does it claim that a reader will magically transform into a healthy, fulfilled human being. What it can do is to provide an introductory map to assist a reader on his or her personal quest -- not for ultimate answers -- but toward an inner understanding of oneself and learning how to communicate with others more effectively. Personology allows us a glimpse at the possibilities on how to get in touch with who we are, rather than buying into a commercial image. Men, unlike women, haven't usually allowed themselves the opportunity to explore their inner selves. They have been caught up in performing what is expected of them.

Organization of the Book

The traits described in this book are grouped loosely into four areas, which are described in the next four Chapters.

Physical Traits   are associated with physical situations such as whether a person is built

	physically to sit or stand for long periods of time.
Automatic Expression	traits are more spontaneous, e.g., Emotional Expressiveness and Impulsiveness.
Feelings and Emotions	involve feelings such as Self-Confidence and Tolerance.
Thinking Traits	involve the way we process information, e.g. the need to analyze and critique it, to review it step by step or race to conclusions.

By examining each of these four areas, a primary personality comes into focus. The traits by themselves predict behavioral patterns. However, as previously discussed, when combined with other traits the effects may be modified or reinforced. The combination of traits gives each individual a better perspective of themselves and others. Instead of being regarded as strange and not "fitting the norm" we point out the behavior that is normal for that individual, and it's really okay.

As you read the following chapters and begin to focus on single traits in isolation, keep in mind that each individual trait must be seen in context with other characteristics. It is also important to remember a person's overall style, approach to life and basic motivations. This book does not offer a "do-it-yourself" profile. It is intended as a guide to understand recognizable features in the face and assist in effective interaction and communication. In order to have an accurate career or personality profile, it is necessary to consult with a certified personologist. There is much more work to be done in the field of linking the structure/function relationship.

The traits included in this book have been tested on thousands of people and found to be 92 percent accurate. To locate a consultant in your area, please send your inquiries to the address given at the end of the book. We will now explore some of these concepts. You will find it easier to practice your new found knowledge on others, since it is harder to be objective about oneself. Study one trait at a time until you have fully mastered each concept. You may want to begin with photographs of family and friends.

*If we do not know what port we are steering for,
no wind is favorable.*

- Seneca

PHYSICAL TRAITS

- Foot Dexterity   19
- Hand Dexterity   23
- Risk Taking   26
- Philosophical Trend   29
- Physical Insulation   30
- Serious Mindedness   36
- Physicalness   37

The one thing in the world of value,
is the active soul.

- Emerson

FOOT DEXTERITY

This is not a skill in kicking field goals, but the measurement of how long the legs are in proportion to the body. This basic ratio determines where the center of gravity is, and whether a person is built to sit or stand comfortably most of the time. The leg length will have a direct bearing on the career selection and the individual's physical needs of expression in sport activities and daily life. People who have a medium length have the ability to both sit and stand for reasonable length of time. They need to balance their activities more. If we were to study the facial features and foot dexterity in relationship to the sport activity, we would probably notice a strong correlation between those observations and the level of skill for that particular sport. There are some American football teams where the players are actually measured to assess their value as a player. There are of course other traits that can make up for the less developed trait needed for a particular activity. Such as the degree of physicalness within the individual.

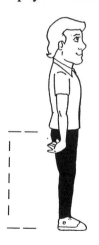

Figure 1   *High Foot Dexterity*   *Low Foot Dexterity*

Low Foot Dexterity

People with short torsos and long legs (high center of gravity) do their best thinking and working in a sitting position, such as desk jobs or an activity which takes them off their feet. They are not built to be on their legs for long periods of time. Should they find themselves in jobs that require standing for long periods of time, they need to give themselves a break at least every two hours. Or, find a stool to sit on if the individual serves at the counter. Waiters and waitresses who are long legged, often develop back problems partly due to standing all day. Long legged individuals often take after the male side of the family.

Recommended sport activities could be basketball, kayaking, swimming, tai-chi, ice skating, horseback riding and touring in a car. Related careers would include computer programming, accounting, sewing, receptionist, truck or taxi cab driver.

High Foot Dexterity

People built with a long torso and short legs (low center of gravity) will have an easier time standing and working on their feet. Sitting for long periods of time makes them restless. A person in sales had been reassigned to a desk job and expressed how much he disliked that position. His shorter legs were part of the reason. Another reason was he needed people contact. If sitting is part of the job requirement, try to get some exercise either before the day starts or during the lunch hour.

Problem solving or stress reduction activities are best done when individuals with this trait go for a walk. Try to select an environment where you feel the most relaxed such as by the water, out in the open space or in a wooded setting. Physical activities could include hiking, jogging, running, tennis, soccer, football, gardening, aerobics, wrestling, mountain climbing. Related careers, depending of course on other traits, would include sales, construction, architecture, beautician, nursing, restaurant work, gardening, military officer or any job that requires standing.

Directing Low Foot Dexterity

Select a career which allows you to be off your feet. If you are in a job that requires standing all day, make sure you take short rest periods. If possible, find a seat and rest your legs. When on a vacation, plan a mixture of touring and physical activities. Make sure your travel companions are of similar build. If not, work something out ahead of time so that the activities are compatible with both parties.

Application to relationships. Understanding the physical build of another person will avoid disappointment when engaging in activities which are in conflict with the other persons build. Find a way to reach a compromise. For example, you are on a tour and your companion(s) have short legs. Take frequent stops to allow them to stretch their legs. Or, if you have plans to take a 12 mile hike, check with them first to find out if they can handle the distance, then allow frequent rest stops. This will avoid the disappointment of cutting the trip short. What can happen is the other person may be putting up with the discomfort and not really enjoying the activity. When two people have a similar build, their time together will be heightened by their mutual enjoyment.

Children generally develop their proportions by time they reach kindergarten. The child with a longer torso can be distinguished at birth. The parents should guide their children into activities designed for this body type. By observing this trait early it will help avoid frustrations and disappointment by the child. Note that if the child is short legged they will have a harder time sitting still. Try to make sure they get a certain amount of activity throughout the day.

Directing High Foot Dexterity

When you are feeling restless, take a walk or get some physical exercise. This will maintain a balance through the day. Exercise is a good activity for solving problems or mood shifts. Learn to recognize this trait in others. If you are vacationing with friends who are on the opposite pole, understand they will need rest periods between activities. Or, if you are in a situation where there are long periods of being on foot, suggest a coffee break. Your time will be more productive.

HAND DEXTERITY

Manual dexterity is found by the similarity in the length of the three middle fingers. With your palms facing you and the fingers together, take a look at your three middle fingers. Are they similar in length or dissimilar? Which hand, left or right, has the fingers which are closer in length? This will indicate whether you are left or right handed. Sometimes both hands can be the same, in which case this individual is possibly ambidextrous.

Figure 2   Low Hand Dexterity   *Hight Hand Dexterity*

High Hand Dexterity

People with high hand dexterity have more innate skill when working with their hands, since they can grasp and manipulate objects more effectively. Individuals who have this trait are said to be "clever with their hands". People who do not have this trait find they work harder to achieve the same results. However, if they are good at assembling parts together, this will add to their ability to use their hands for making jewelry or stained glass window work. This explains why some people love to work with their hands while others never show any particular interest. When individuals who score high on this trait engage in activities with their hands such as sculpture, massage or playing a musical instrument, they experience deep feelings and satisfaction. This experience is heightened when an individual has additional traits such as fine hair (which indicates sensitivity), rounded ears (a high sense of rhythm) and straight eyebrows (suggesting a high appreciation of the esthetics).

Directing High Hand Dexterity

People with high Hand Dexterity have a natural ability to work with their hands. It requires less effort for them to achieve good results. Use this ability for either a hobby or as a vocation.

Vocations where this trait could be applied would be massage therapist, chiropractor, physical therapy, dentistry, hair design (with high design appreciation) carpentry, art and crafts, fine jeweler or playing a musical instrument.

Directing Low Hand Dexterity

The person with low hand dexterity does not have the "natural" ability of the high score. They will have to work harder to achieve the same results. A color analysis student who had low hand dexterity, was asked to cut fabric swatches in half. She found it very challenging to make a straight cut. It was suggested that in her own business this activity should be delegated to someone else. Recognizing that not everyone is a natural "handy man" and focusing on each individuals natural abilities will lead to more precision in the work place and home.

Learning to identify this trait in children will greatly help them to develop their innate skills. Buying them toys that require high hand dexterity and precision could prove to be challenging. Support and acknowledge them when they achieve results even though those results may not come up to the parents expectations.

Eyedness/Handedness

Eyedness and handedness are inherent. In the natural pattern, the individual who is right-handed will also be right-eyed. The reverse is true if the person is naturally left handed and left-eyed. Serious maladjustments may occur if the native handedness is changed during later childhood The natural flow from brain to expression and from nerve reception to brain impression will be impeded. When there is such a mixture with left and right we call this, in personology, mixed dominance. Because of this conflict, such a person functions at cross-purposes in simple tasks, such as cutting bread or fabric. You will notice they cut on the slant, because they are sighting with one eye and slicing with the opposite hand.

To test which eye is dominant, stretch out your arm with both eyes open. With your index finger sight your eyes on a small round object across the room. Now close one eye. Does your finger stay on the object without making any adjustments? Or does it jump? The master eye will stay focused on the object. However, the master eye can change if the person develops astigmatism. They will notice the dominant eye will change and sometimes with this change the individual may notice they start reversing letters or start a sentence with the second letter.

Spatulated and Tapered Fingers

This is observed by the squareness on the end of the fingers which indicates they have the ability to work fine precision with their hands. Sometimes this spatulation is caused by the finger tips being in constant contact with a flat surface such as computer keyboard, sculpture, pottery, playing a musical instrument, dental or mechanical work. When the ends of the fingers are tapered, this also indicates the individual will look best in blue based red and those whose fingers are rounded or square will look better in yellow based reds. This information has been observed on thousands of color clients and found to be extremely accurate. It does not indicate which red but in most cases determines whether the red they can wear is yellow or blue based.

Risk Taking

Risk taking correlates with the length of the ring finger compared with the index finger. This is best viewed with the palm of the hand facing you and the fingers touching each other. If the ring finger is longer this suggests this individual enjoys taking a risk, risk gives them a natural high. If there is a difference between the two hands in the finger measurement, this indicates someone comfortable taking risks and at other times being more conservative. When the ring finger is shorter than the index finger this indicates a more cautious nature, and if risks are taken they are calculated risks.

Risk taking could be anything from adrenaline releasing physical activities like skydiving, to more intellectual and passive ventures such as speculating in the stock market or gambling. Sometimes people are willing to risk all, without considering the consequences.

An individual who wound up in prison for a short term drug sentence, loved to race motor cycles. While in this confined environment he realized that drugs were a way of dealing with his frustration of not being challenged by taking risks. Recognizing this need, he later made sure he engaged in activities such as racing, rock climbing and sky diving, which gave him the risk element he needed to lead a balanced life.

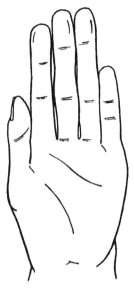

Figure 3   *Risk Taking*

High Risk Taking

People who score high on risk taking enjoy the thrill that comes with taking chances. It is important to recognize this trait in teenagers, or they may direct this need into a negative direction such as buying and selling drugs or theft. Channel their energies into sports or other activities which have an element of risk, the reward for them is the exhilarating experience. This is hard for parents whose traits indicate a more cautious nature. When we recognize and support these needs in our children, it will help to guide them through the more challenging years.

Low Risk Taking

When people are more conservative, the risks are more calculated. They will consider all aspects of a situation before taking a chance. They will put their financial investments into a secure market. Sometimes this conservative approach can hold people back from achieving their goals or changing career directions. A risk for these people could be changing jobs, living in a new city or participating in a new activity. This may appear dull to those people who are natural risk takers. However, low risk takers are operating out of their own comfort zone. Risk taking is on a different level for them.

Directing Low Risk Taking

If you are very conservative, experience taking a risk now and again, it will help to stretch your perceived limitations. If there is some element of risk, familiarize yourself with what it entails. This will help you approach the situation with more confidence. Don't dampen the enthusiasm of people who are seekers of the unknown.

How to Direct High Risk Taking

Consider how the risk could effect other people's lives. Participate in a sport or other activities which satisfy the need to take chances. Do not expect low risk takers to eagerly embrace your passion for risk. If you enjoy gambling, make sure you keep within your budget, particularly if you have family responsibilities. Many relationships have been effected by out of control gambling.

A note to parents, if your children want to engage in activities that appear high risk, make sure they have the training needed prior to their participation. In this way you will feel more relaxed and the chances of being injured will hopefully be reduced.

PHILOSOPHICAL TREND

This trait was first identified by the Egyptians around 3000 BC. It was observed there was a strong correlation between the gaps in the fingers and philosophical tendencies. When the palms are viewed with the fingers together against the light, there is a certain amount of space visible between the fingers where the light shines through.

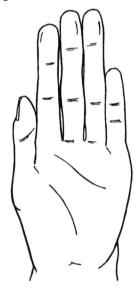   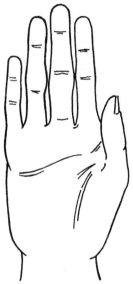

Figure 4   Low Philosophical Trend   *High Philosophical Trend*

Significant gaps show a more philosophical person who may look for the deeper meaning in life. When there is no gaping between the fingers, this shows little or no interest in philosophical tendencies. People with a strong philosophical trend are continually searching for answers to their life purpose. They are restless until they get a sense of their own balance and harmony. They have an innate sense for spiritual values and seek a purpose beyond material levels. These people may go on a lifelong personal quest to seek a lifestyle that gives them a deeper meaning and satisfaction. There is an inner awareness that seeks tranquillity. They need to get in touch with themselves on a spiritual level. They may go on retreats or travel to India to study under a guru to find their answers. The Chinese have linked this trait to gambling, however the observation was found to be inconsistent with this trait. Interests include the pursuit of evangelistic and philosophical issues and metaphysics. Occupations include the ministry, leading philosophical workshops and seminars.

Directing a Philosophical Trend

Attend, or offer, workshops on philosophical, spiritual or religious interests. Learn to keep personal beliefs in perspective. Be willing to listen and understand other people's viewpoints on philosophical or religious discussions. Recognize that the basis of all religions is to love thy neighbor and to offer support to others in need.

PHYSICAL INSULATION

Physical Insulation indicates a person's insulation to external circumstances such as sound, touch, taste, feelings and environment. This measurement is taken from the thickness of a hair shaft (a single strand of hair). The higher the insulation a person has, the "more" of an experience is needed to reach their consciousness. The finer the insulation a person has, the less time is required to respond to the external environment. When individuals are raised in environments that are not native to them, they will develop a certain tolerance to their surroundings. This was the situation for a woman who was raised in a very noisy family. She did not realize how uncomfortable the sound level was until she moved away from home. Upon returning for a visit, she found the noise level was extremely unpleasant and was glad to escape! The same applies to individuals who have coarser hair. If they are brought up in a refined environment they will be more sensitive to others who are opposite to themselves. Training may modify a persons behavior, but it does not create a permanent change.

Figure 5 High Physical Insulation   *Low Physical Insulation*

High Physical Insulation

People with coarser hair need more stimulation to elicit a response. These people are less sensitive to pain. We have the saying when an individual has been the subject of insult or hurt feelings, their response is viewed as "it's water off a duck's back". Coarse haired individuals like things on a grand scale in sound, amounts of food, laughter, stronger sensations and intensity. They love the outdoors, camping and the extreme elements of the sun, wind, rain and snow. It takes longer to get under their skin, and they may appear insensitive to other people's needs. They are much more expressive in their reaction, particularly when they are enthusiastic. During a networking event a coarse haired person volunteered his/her services. This individual became quite excited about the sales they were generating for the fine haired person. The course haired person kept hitting the fine haired person's arm saying in a loud voice, "See how good I am!" The fine haired person felt very bruised and embarrassed at the loudness and aggressive style of selling.

If a person with high physical insulation takes a job that keeps them constantly inside, they will feel a strong need to get outside. When this trait is also combined with green eyes, there will be a strong need to spend some time outdoors. They enjoy camping in the woods. Individuals who live in big cities, have high physical insulation and green eyes may find themselves getting irritated if they do not spend time in the outdoors. This would apply to all individuals with this eye color.

Directing High Physical Insulation

People with high physical insulation are less sensitive to the needs of others. For example, when they are with people who have finer hair, they would be more popular by asking if the music is too loud, or how they can make the camping experience more comfortable. If you have high physical insulation, be aware that others may be more sensitive, and modify your expression and actions. Use a softer tone, be considerate. Think in terms of quality, especially when giving gifts. When you are with people who have similar traits, you can interact with them on the same level. The challenge is to work out good relationships with individuals who are more sensitive. For the sensitive person the coarser haired individual will appear insensitive, loud and without polish. These observations are not necessarily the intended message but that is how it is being interpreted. High physical insulated individuals should learn how to temper their actions when with those who are more sensitive. Think more about the needs of others.

Low Physical Insulation

Individuals with fine hair become quickly irritated when people around them are coarse or loud. Individuals with fine hair prefer quality rather than quantity. To these people quality means everything, from fine pieces of furniture to delicate china. Elegant dining and traveling in comfort. To others they will appear to be overly sensitive and will be made fun of through the lack of understanding. Their feelings get hurt very quickly and they may internalize these feelings for days. Often times they will be so focused on what has happened that it will take over their lives. This was the case for an individual who was going through some personal challenges in her life. Just by changing her focus she was able to wake up the next morning feeling like a load was lifted off her shoulders. Fine haired individuals are much quicker to react to "outside" influences. Camping out in the rough is not as enjoyable as staying in a bed and breakfast for the night. They thrive in a more protective environment. In general they are not campers, however if the camping situation has sufficient comforts then it may be more acceptable.

Directing Low Physical Insulation

If you have low physical insulation understand that others are not intending to hurt or offend you. In addition, if you have low tolerance and a tendency to be very emotional, you are inclined to over react. When this occurs, consciously choose to be in control of your reactions. When other people seem loud or rough, notice if their hair is coarse. Understanding another person's trait will enable you to react in an appropriate way. You may need to adjust your reactions or remove yourself from the environment. Learn how to tune out what is going on around you. Remind yourself it's your fine hair and possibly high emotions that are causing you to feel so hurt. Learn to focus outside of the problem by getting involved with another activity. Listen to what people are saying, not the way they are saying it. Remember the remarks that hurt your feelings were not necessarily the intention of the individual. It was how you interpreted the communication.

People who have hair that is of medium thickness will find they are able to adapt easily to what is around them, they are more easily able to give and take. Just being more aware of others helps them know which way to interact with them. When an individual has a mixture of both fine and coarse hair they will find themselves going back and forth in their moods. One moment they will want the sound turned up and another time they will like it quieter. When caught up in an emotional set of circumstances, a higher degree of sensitivity will be set off. Everything that seemed right before will now appear wrong. They'll become more irritated and wonder why they are feeling this way. They perceive something must be wrong with them. This perception will last until the system relaxes, then the mood will pass. When these mood swings occur take up enjoyable activities that will help you stabilize such as listening to your favorite music, stepping outside, going for a walk or a bike ride.

Relationships

Ideally two individuals who live together should have similar physical insulation. If there are wide differences there may be a greater misunderstanding and hurt feelings. Couples are often times forgiving of each others traits during the courting stages, but afterwards the differences are no longer tolerable. Should one person have coarse hair and the other fine, the finer person may see the opposite as being rough and harsh. They are more aggressive in their love making when this trait is combined with physicalness (*figure 7*). In turn, the coarser haired individual would think their husband/wife was being overly sensitive and complaining. Once this trait is understood by both parties, they can individually make the necessary behavior adjustments. Couples who are contemplating living together, should go through a personology counseling prior to that commitment. It would save a lot of hurt feelings, time and money. Why go through the pain of trial and error when a small investment of time and money may save those painful emotions?

Children

Children with fine hair need to learn how to act with others no matter what their texture is. Help them to understand why they are drawing away from unpleasant sounds, odors or being overly sensitive to hurt feelings. Make sure children with coarser hair have time to play in the outdoors. Teach them how to modulate their voices, not be so rowdy around others with finer hair and to be aware of each others needs. When there are differences between parent and child, one being coarse and the other fine, make sure communication is not misunderstood. An example would be a father who has coarse hair and a son who has fine hair. The father may see his son as being overly sensitive and behaving like a sissy. Once the father understands the differences between their traits, he will be able to avoid negative communication and hurt feelings. If the child has coarse hair, be firm with him/her. Speak in a loud firm voice. This is especially true with teenagers. Teach them to accept others as they are and not to pass judgment.

SERIOUS MINDEDNESS

Deep-set eyes show Serious Mindedness. People with this trait take life, work and responsibilities extremely serious. They may not always see the more humorous side of life. When you give these people a job to do, it will be well done.

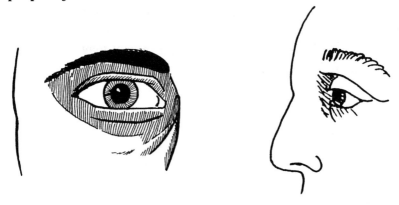

Figure 6   Serious Mindedness

Trait Combinations
The effect of Serious Mindedness will be amplified should an individual have low tolerance, fine hair and spend a lot of time thinking through information. People with this combination are inclined to be more thoughtful and reflective. Small issues become more significant and completely absorb them.

Directing Serious Mindedness
To create a more balanced life, Serious Minded people need to develop a lighter side and learn not to take life so seriously. They need to take up a hobby or physical activity to help them relax and have fun. They tend to carry the world on their shoulders. Public

figures with this trait include; Cher, Nancy Reagan, Abraham Lincoln and Ghandi.

PHYSICALNESS

The bony protuberance at the back of the head (the cerebellum) indicates the need for physical activity. It also indicates how quickly a person is physically stimulated. This physical drive is expressed both mentally and through physical activity.

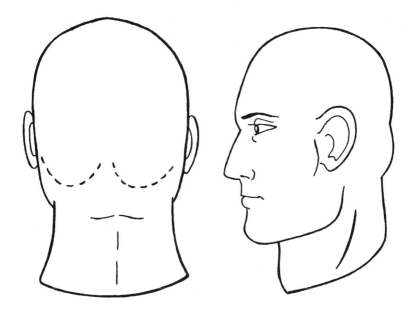

Figure 7   High Physicalness

High Physicalness

Once people with this trait get an idea or goal, they want to immediately put it into action. These are the people who move the piano instead of the stool. They enjoy physical activities, and exercise needs to be a part of their daily routine, otherwise they become restless and irritable.

Low Physicalness

People who score low on Physicalness enjoy being spectators rather than being physically involved. To others they may appear to be lazy and boring, particularly when this trait is combined with long legs (*figure 1*). People who score low on these two traits may be called "couch potatoes" when biologically they do not feel an urgent physical need for exercise. They're quite comfortable being at home, enjoying a good book or watching their favorite television program. They do not have the same physical stamina or staying power as the people who have a higher score on Physicalness. This could be a problem in a relationship if the other person is on the opposite pole. One would want to be active while the other is quite happy to sit in a chair.

Trait Combinations

This trait is amplified when combined with Physical Motive (*figure 32*). People with both these traits are very enthusiastic people and pour energy into everything they do.

People with Physical Motive (*figure 32*), Forcefulness and high Physicalness provide a driving force in getting projects started and completed. They want it done now. If their traits also include low Self-Confidence, then in the eagerness to get things finished, they may not do a thorough job. These are very intense people who find it hard to relax. They are much happier kept busy otherwise they become quickly bored. This is an advantage when there are projects waiting to be started.

Directing Low Physicalness

Make sure you take some time to exercise during the day. When with others who are more physical, make sure you have had plenty of rest the day before.

Directing High Physicalness

Take up hobbies that involve physical activity. Understand that not everyone likes to move at the same pace.

AUTOMATIC EXPRESSION TRAITS

- Authoritative   43
- Self-Reliance   47
- Tenacity   48
- Pioneering Trend   51
- Adventurous   53
- Automatic Giving   55
- Pride in Personal Appearance   57
- Dry Wit   58
- Automatic Resistance   59
- Administrative/Ministrative   62
- Concise/Verbose   64
- Impulsiveness   67
- Credulity/Skepticism   69

How can I be useful,
of what service can I be?

There is something inside me,
what can it be?

-Vincent Van Gogh

AUTHORITATIVE

The Authoritative trait is indicated by the width of the jaw in comparison to the width of the Self-Confidence line (*figure 22*). When the jaw line is wider than the Self-Confidence line, the individual is very authoritative, whereas a narrow jaw indicates this person is less authoritative.

 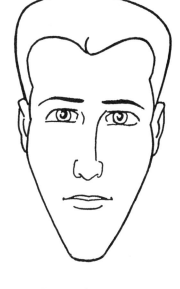

Figure 8 High Authoritativeness   *Low Authoritativeness*

The appearance of authority and of being in command is also enhanced by the quality and tone of the voice. These individuals have a commanding nature and sound very convincing. It's very difficult for them to take a back seat, when others are floundering.

People with width at the outer edge of the eye line (high Self-Confidence, *figure 22*) and jaw appear authoritative and powerful. They are decisive, and do well both in communication and action. They gain respect from others, and because of their decisive tone, manner and total lack of doubt, they appear in command. Examples would be General Swartzkopf, Diane Feinstein and not surprisingly The Duchess of York, who I am sure found it very challenging at times to take a more submissive role.

People with this trait may be annoying to some because they appear as "know it all's", when the behavior is not in check. They can quite unintentionally take over a conversation or discussion through their authoritativeness, although their intent was to draw it out. The appearance of too much authority can be intimidating, to others, causing concern or discomfort about expressing a different viewpoint or conflicting information. This becomes a problem when there are several authoritative people in a group, they all want to have their say and take over. When these individuals are engaged in a strong discussion, because each wants to be heard, their voices will become louder and louder as they talk over each other. This makes it very difficult for others to follow a conversation and is less productive. Authoritative figures need to consciously allow each person to make their statement without interruption and invite others to take the lead in a discussion.

Employees of a large aerospace company were having a problem with their new boss. This person was very Authoritative, High Self-Confident and Forceful. When she wore her bright red outfit, she was perceived as very aggressive and extremely intimidating. It was tactfully suggested that she wear a softer color at the next employee meeting, a color that would subdue the natural authority she exuded. The results spoke for themselves. When people are physically Authoritative, they need to learn when stronger or softer colors are more appropriate.

The people who are low on the authoritative trait appear to be less decisive or not very strong in their convictions. Their voices are softer and sound more diplomatic. They need to cultivate a tone of authoritativeness and act with definite intent. When low authority features are combined with fine hair, this person needs to raise the volume of the voice, deepen the tone, and use bigger gestures to give the appearance of authority. This is very important when giving lectures or workshops. In a situation when a stronger statement will be needed, wearing deeper, stronger colors will support the position. Usually Low Authoritative people are easy to talk to, depending on other traits. They exchange ideas and information more readily, and treat each other as equals. Examples are Bill Clinton (high Authoritativeness) versus Prince Charles (low Authoritativeness).

Trait Combinations
When other trait combinations are evident with low Authoritativeness, such as sharp features and a forceful personality, this overcomes the lack of authority to make the appearance more aggressive. For example, Ross Perot, Marcia Clark (Prosecuting attorney for the O.J. Simpson trial) and John McEnroe.

Directing Authoritativeness
Unless you are actually in charge, let others take the lead. Use a softer tone when needed. You may be set off by being challenged. When you sense conflict coming on try not to appear argumentative, stay calm and assess the situation. Wearing formal colors strengthens your authority, which may be intimidating. Using softer colors or clothes that have prints will open discussion, whether one on one, or in a group session. When working with people who are both Authoritative and Forceful, do not try to force

them to back down. Discuss the issue with them, use a more subtle approach by which their ego is not diminished.

Directing Low Authoritativeness

Cultivate a more definite and decisive tone of voice and use stronger gestures. Take a firm stand when you are being challenged and speak with confidence. Let people know that you are knowledgeable. When you are in a leadership position, it is very important to create the right first impression. To increase your authority, wear more formal colors. Use larger gestures when describing something or making a point. Practice in front of a mirror or better still, ask someone to video your presentation. If you give a lot of presentations, enroll in a public speaking class or speaking circle. Buy a pair of glasses (even if they are not needed), the frame adds strength to the facial design.

SELF-RELIANCE

This is indicated by how much the nostrils flare out from the nose. The greater the flare the higher the Self-Reliance. People with high Self-Reliance know how to use their own inner resources to get things done, or overcome adversity. If they were lost in the desert, they would have a strong sense that they would find their way out. Their inner conversation is "I know I can do it." They instinctively know how to handle different situations and do not feel they have to lean on others for support.

Figure 9   Low Self-Reliance   *High Self-Reliance*

People with low Self-Reliance may be too dependent on others for decisions and direction. They do not always give themselves credit for what they know. Their inner conversation is one of questioning whether they will succeed. When confronted with new situations they recall all the times when things have worked against them. They will appear hesitant to start a project or take a trip by themselves. For example, they gather all the information for starting a business or project, but then not follow through when a situation occurs that puts doubt in their minds.

Trait Combinations
When low Self-Reliance is combined with low Self-Confidence, these individuals may rely heavily on other people to handle projects. However they are more than willing to accept advice and follow directions.

Directing High Self-Reliance
People with high Self-Reliance are very independent and prefer to tackle a job their way rather than follow others. This may alienate them from the team. If you have high Self-Reliance, recognize when it can work for or against you.

Directing Low Self-Reliance
Learn to make your own decisions. Think things through before you get involved in new situations. Write out the steps needed to achieve the best results, at the end, acknowledge your achievement. Note how much you have learned by relying on your own decisions, whether it was positive or negative. Before taking on a project, take a deep breath and tell yourself you can do it. Do not dwell on your past failures, this will inhibit your growth. Try to take on the task by yourself before asking others for their input.

TENACITY

This is indicated by the amount of chin protruding forward when viewed from the side profile. The more it protrudes forward, the more Tenacious the person is. A receding chin indicates less Tenacity.

When individuals with high tenacity get their teeth into a project or relationship, they hang on till the bitter end. They have a tendency to hold onto what they are doing, right or wrong. When working with these individuals ask them to define what their goals are. Then you can assess if they are on the right track and beneficial to the overall plan. Examples are, Robin Williams, Marlon Brando, John Tesh and The Duchess of York.

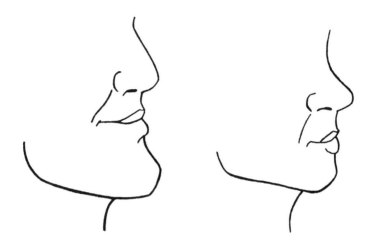

*Figure 10   High Tenacity (Protruding chin)
Low Tenacity (chin recedes)*

Directing High Tenacity

If you are a person with high Tenacity, you may fail to recognize that what you are doing is no longer working. Know when it's time to let go, rather than hanging on hoping things will work out. Hang on for the right reasons, but do not go down with the ship. Let go if what you are doing does not play into your long term goal.

Directing Low Tenacity

People with less Tenacity will "let go" of a situation, when there is no advantage to "hanging on". They are, however, more willing

49

to find another way around the problem. Before starting a new project or venture, set goals. Define what you really want to happen before tackling the problem. Then you will know whether to hang on, and why. When you find yourself confused and ready to back off a situation, stop and review your goals. If they are right then don't let go, create another approach. Your challenge is to look and act mentally strong on the outside. An example of low tenacity is Prince Charles.

PIONEERING TREND

This trait is shown by the straightness of the outside rim (helix) of the ear. People with this trait have an entrepreneurial spirit. They like to explore new territory and start new projects and ventures. These are the visionaries that have a burning desire to be the first to venture into a new field. They do better when working for themselves. Examples would be Dr. Martin Luther King, Bill Gates, Steve Jobs and Margaret Thatcher.

Figure 11   High Pioneering Trend

Trait Combinations

When the Pioneering Trend is combined with high Tolerance (*figure 23*) and Construction (*figure 41*) the result may be taking on too many new projects, instead of staying focused. When this trait is less evident on individuals, they do not have such a strong urge to break into new territory. If we were able to take a peek back into history, we might well observe definite patterns in the facial structure that reflected the pioneering spirit of the time.

Directing a Pioneering Trend

When you find yourself becoming stagnant, look for new areas that will stimulate your creativity. Remember to stay focused or you may find your efforts diluted by too many projects. Keep a journal and write down all of your ideas, then look for the patterns and how those ideas relate to each other. Those that do not make sense toss out. This exercise will assist you in formulating a plan of action.

ADVENTUROUS

This trait is indicated by how much the cheek bones protrude from the sides and front of the face. Individuals with prominent cheek bones love adventure and need to have constant change in their daily life. They want to be where things are happening and get physical excitement from new experiences. They enjoy variety in their day, and love to travel. In repetitive situations they are quickly bored.

Figure 12   *High Adventurousness*

Those with high Adventurous traits need variety in their day, particularly if they are also High Tolerance (*figure 23*). Doing the same thing day after day becomes very boring to them. The Adventurous child needs constant change and excitement. If this is not found, they may get into mischief just for the thrill of it. Involve them in sports or hobbies where they show a strong interest. Make sure their day has a variety of activities. Examples of those with high Adventurousness are Hillary Clinton, Sophia Loren, Princess Diana, Newt Gingrich and Barbara Walters. People who score low on Adventurousness are more content to stay at home. It may cause a problem in a marriage when one person scores high on adventurous and the other low. One will want to be on the move and the other will prefer to stay with what feels familiar. Adventurous people will feel that others who are less adventurous are missing out on the excitement. However, the less Adventurous derive their enjoyment from the quality of the experience itself, rather than the excitement it brings.

Directing Low Adventurousness

In order not to be misunderstood by those who are more adventurous, be willing to venture out in your life. Get into the spirit of the moment and share their excitement. At the same time the adventurous person should learn to share with you those moments when you would prefer to stay close to home.

Directing Adventurousness

Sometimes people who are high in Adventurousness become very restless. They may confuse their nomadic spirit with the need to live in many different locations. If you score high on this trait, use your free time to travel, or take up a hobby that gives you the variety you need. Remember that not everyone shares your same enthusiasm for change. Make sure you set aside some time to spend with your significant other. This could be a challenge in relationships if one person wants to be on the move and the other prefers to stay at home. If this is an issue in your relationship, discuss how you can arrange time together to avoid the feeling of being tied to the home. Don't change for change sake or use it as an escape to avoid reality. This seems to be a challenge for single people, they feel that a commitment to marriage will cramp their style and curtail their freedom.

Possible careers are flight attendant (notice the next time you fly how many attendants have this trait), travel agent, commissioned sales, international marketing, advertising, theater (with Forward Balance).

AUTOMATIC GIVING

This trait is determined by the size of the lower lip in comparison to the size of the face. The larger the lip, the greater the generosity.

Figure 13   High Automatic Giving

People who score high on Automatic Giving have a tendency to over extend themselves both in time and money. They take on more than they can handle. They find it hard to receive gifts from others and will appear that they are not open to receiving. Other people may rely heavily on them for both their time and financial resources. Learn when to say no before over extending yourself and only give what you can reasonably afford, whether it is time or possessions. People with this trait, combined with Impulsiveness (*figure 19*) and Low Acquisitiveness may give away their last penny.

People who score low on Automatic Giving give more consideration in the act of giving. They may appear stingy, tight to others or they may be seen as using and abusing other people's generosity. Sometimes they feel the act of just giving is rather frivolous and unnecessary. They may also find it difficult to express their inner feelings within a relationship or family. Underneath their feelings they may be strong even though they appear to close themselves off from others.

Directing High Automatic Giving

Allow others the pleasure of giving to you. Knowing the pleasure you receive from the act of giving allows others an opportunity to be grateful and appreciative towards you. When you refuse gifts, or show a lack of enthusiasm, it will deeply hurt the givers feelings and make them feel rejected. Think before you give or offer your services without charge. Don't let people take advantage of you.

Directing Low Automatic Giving

Learn to give to others without any strings attached. Give more of yourself in personal relationships, and spend more time helping others who would greatly appreciate your assistance. Express your feelings more, surprise your significant other with a bouquet of flowers or their favorite bottle of wine. Open up your feelings to your children and express how much you care about them. Make sure you are available to them.

PRIDE IN PERSONAL APPEARANCE

This is shown by the shortness of the upper lip. The shorter it is, the stronger the need to look good and get attention based on appearance. Consequently, these people enjoy clothes and may have an extensive wardrobe. They have a natural ability for creating attractive clothing combinations. This trait is often seen in designers, personal shoppers and sales assistants in clothing departments. Individuals with this trait may appear to be extremely vain, and can't go by a mirror without checking their appearance. They will also be very conscious of slight blemishes or scars and will invest a lot of money to correct what they see as glaring imperfections. They are also inclined to take things personally and do not accept criticism well. If this applies to you, listen to the content of the conversation rather than focus on the negative reaction.

Figure 14   Pride in personal appearance

If children have this trait, involve them with the purchasing of their clothes and encourage them to select what to wear that day.

Teach them how to identify the difference in the quality of clothing and how to create different color combinations.

Trait Combinations
When Pride in Personal Appearance is combined with fine hair, esthetics and design appreciation (the top of the eyebrow has an inverted V) a person with these traits may enjoy a career as a clothing designer, interior design or image consultant.

Directing Pride in Personal Appearance
Do not take it personally if your work comes under criticism. The person who is making the comments may have good intentions, although their opinion was not solicited.

DRY WIT

Dry wit is indicated by the long upper lip. When the length above the lip is longer in comparison to the size of the face, this indicates a dry sense of humor. This trait reflects the opposite of Pride in Personal Appearance.

People who have this trait are more concerned with getting the job done, rather than how they look. When they dress in the morning, they would much rather put on comfortable clothes than get all dressed up. They are less interested in the current clothing trends, and are the personal shoppers' dream clients because there is so much potential to reach. These individuals get so wrapped up in what they're doing that dressing is the last thing on their minds.

Figure 15   Dry Wit   A Dry sense of Humor

Directing Direct Dry Wit

Never use your dry wit on anyone in a way that could cause hurt feelings. When buying clothes, hire a personal shopper, this will save you time and money in the long run. It will also make the shopping experience an enjoyable one rather than one of necessity.

AUTOMATIC RESISTANCE

A more accurate term for this trait is stubbornness. People whose jaws look wedge shaped (pointed chin) automatically resist under any pressure. They appear to handle pressure much better than most. However, because they keep things bottled up inside them, while seemingly handling a situation, they often eventually experience medical problems from internalizing the stress they are under. When an individual with this trait has low tolerance and are very emotional they will express their frustrations more dramatically.

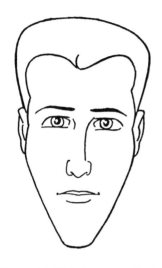 

Figure 16 High Automatic Resistance   *Low Automatic Resistance*

When people with high Automatic Resistance are pushed into action, they will put up strong resistance and automatically say no when they feel pressure. The more they are pushed the more they will dig into the ground and refuse to move. When this trait is in a young child, explain to them the benefits gained by doing something rather than saying "You have to, that's why". When you give children (as well as adults) a choice and motivating reasons they will come around. Ross Perot, Julia Roberts and Prince Charles are good examples of high Automatic Resistance.

When the jaw is less pointed, people tend to be more agreeable and complian at the moment. They give in more easily to pressure or persuasion, although that does not mean they like what is happening. Generally they tend to avoid confrontation and try to think their way around a situation. Low Automatic Resistance is indicated when the point of the chin is very square. People who have this trait tend to be more pugnacious. They enjoy a good meaty discussion which may be perceived by others as argumentative. Generally they are more compliant and work well under pressure.

Directing High Automatic Resistance

When dealing with people who have high Automatic Resistance, do not apply pressure. Discuss the situation at hand. Find out the reason for their objection or belief. These people do not like being forced into situations. Use a more persuasive approach, rather than a forceful one, or you will find yourself running into a wall of resistance.

If you are a person with High Automatic Resistance, consider a situation before automatically saying no. What are you gaining by being stubborn without justification? Ask yourself what it is that you are resisting? Is it based on principle or feelings?

Directing Low Automatic Resistance

People with low Automatic Resistance are usually easier to get along with and easier to influence. They are more open and cooperative. If you have low Automatic Resistance, make it known how you feel when the pressure is negative. If the pressure seems overwhelming, just take a moment and see what can be done immediately. Make a plan for completing the project. Make an effort and do what is needed to be done at the moment.

ADMINISTRATIVE versus MINISTRATIVE

The straight or hooked (convex) nose shows an Administrative nature, whereas when the ridge of the nose (next to the eyes) dips down, ski nose, (concave) this indicates a Ministrative nature.

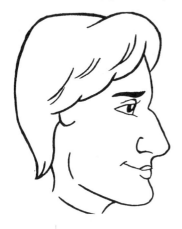 

Figure 17   Administrative   Ministrative
                  Convex   Concave

Administrative people like to oversee a project rather than to ministrate (i.e. to serve). They do not enjoy a job where they are in service such as waiting, nursing, sales assistant, or at the beck and call of others. They prefer to hire and organize the services of others rather than do the job themselves, especially when that means being subservient to others. They are good at delegating.

Administratives are concerned with the best price. They are bargain hunters, value is extremely important to them. This does not necessarily imply they will settle for an inferior product. They may appear to put a price tag on everything, because that is how they make their buying decision. Possible careers would be financial investments, economist, real estate, stock brokerage, business administration and raising money for charities.

Ministrative people are more spontaneous and enjoy helping others. They are the people who like to volunteer and often times over extend themselves particularly if they have automatic giving. They love "to do" for others, helping with whatever needs to be done. When others turn down their offer to help they take it personally. They get so caught up with providing services to others that they forget to serve themselves. Ministrative people find it difficult to charge for their services, consequently they do not place a high value on being paid. They need to learn how to delegate and charge for their services. A book that puts the issues around money into perspective is *"The Trick to Money is Having Some"* by *Stuart Wilde*. Very entertaining and well worth reading.

This particular trait is more fully developed when a child is in their mid to late teens. Encourage your children to start a savings account, teach them early how to handle their money.

Trait Combinations

When high Administrativeness is combined with Acquisitiveness (*figure 38*) these people hold on to their investments. They put money and business first. Examples of high Administration are Margaret Thatcher, Dustin Hoffman, Aristotle Onasis and Ross Perot.

Combine Ministrativeness with high tolerance, automatic giving and considerateness and these individuals may find their services get abused due to their over willingness to help. When this trait is combined with low acquisitiveness, they tend not to balance the check books. They may give away their last penny and this could be a problem in relationships if the significant other has the opposite of this trait. Money is often the cause of dispute in marriages, and this trait could be the significant factor. Possible careers are nursing, ministry, YMCA, physician, secretary, volunteer work, and waiter/waitress.

Directing Administrativeness

If you are an Administrative person, do not put a price tag on everything. Consider offering your own time and learn to enjoy the reward of helping someone. If you also score low in Automatic Giving (*figure 13*) donate to an organization which you know will invest the money well. When working with High Administrative people, know that they will be more concerned with the price, they'll look for a bargain.

Directing Ministrativeness

Think first before offering your services without charge. Stop wasting your time by personally "doing for others." People will place more value on services when they have to pay for them. Do not overly extend yourself. Remember to save time for yourself and your family. Identify your priorities and delegate tasks out to others. In a relationship money issues could become a problem, so try to stay within the agreed budget when possible. Take a class on financial investments. This will help you to manage your money more effectively, especially if you have low acquisitiveness and high automatic giving.

CONCISE/VERBOSE

This trait is identified by the fullness or thinness of the upper lip. The thinner the upper lip, compared to the lower one, the more Concise a person is, the fuller the upper lip the more Verbose.

This trait shows the brevity of expression. People who score high on this trait are more concise, and may even be perceived as terse in their verbal expression. They come to the point with fewer words and do not like repetitious conversation. Politicians and heads of large companies are good examples of Conciseness, such as Lee Iacoca. They are very specific and direct, and do not like to waste words. This may be interpreted as being short, rude by others or lacking diplomacy. The advantage of concise people is that they can give clear, precise and easy to follow directions. It is also observed as a developed, rather than inherited, trait in people who have had a very hard life (physically or emotionally), making them appear tough. When the mouth is both thin and small, in comparison to the whole design of the face, it indicates extreme introversion and difficulty expressing feelings.

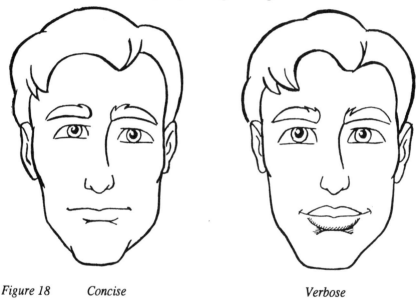

Figure 18   *Concise*   *Verbose*

People who have larger upper lips tend to be more verbose. They are built to express themselves more easily. They embroider conversation with adjectives, adverbs and emotion. Consequently, they may bore others with too much detail. If you ask these people for directions, beware you may get the tour. This verbosity may cause a problem when dealing with people who are more concise, because when given more information than needed, the concise person loses interest in the conversation. They will switch that person off in their mind. The positive aspect of verbosity is that these people can speak at length easily when required. Their speech is more colorful and flowing. They need to avoid repetition or listeners may become bored. Examples of Verbosity are Jimmy Carter, Mick Jagger and Princess Ann.

Trait Combinations

People who are Verbose and Impetuous (lips protruding forward) and are more dramatic in their expression. These people make good story tellers.

Directing Conciseness

If you are a very concise person, interact with others who are more verbose. Embellish your conversation with more adjectives, fill them in with more detail than you would normally use. Ask specific questions, suggest you want to get directly to the point. Try to be patient with verbose people, and listen closely to the content of the conversation. What you are doing is creating a bond by acknowledging others needs. Be more open to express your feelings in detail, so those who are close to you can understand your emotions and decisions. A couple who was on the verge of divorce, decided to have their personology profile made. During the consultation it was revealed that the husband, who had both a thinner upper and lower lip, truly cared about his wife, but had a hard time expressing himself. The last thing he wanted was a divorce. The charts revealed many of the challenges the couple was experiencing. Now they had a tangible tool to work with. It was the turning point in their marriage and today they continue to have a closer relationship and understanding of each other.

Directing Verbose

Be aware of when you are speaking at length. You may lose the person's attention who is more concise. Use fewer words and get to the point. Organize your thoughts before speaking. Sometimes you may find that you talk yourself into or out of a job. Give yourself some space to think things through.

IMPULSIVENESS

The lips are the physical indicator for Impulsiveness. As you look at a person's profile, notice the position of the lips in relation to the glabella (the ridge of the nose). When looking at the profile of the face, do the lips project forward or recede? Take a ruler and line up with the ridge of the nose, making sure the head is level. If the lips from the side profile can be clearly viewed, the person is very impulsive, spontaneous and will jump into any situation without much thought.

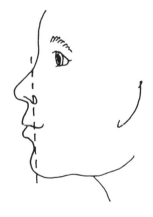
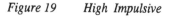
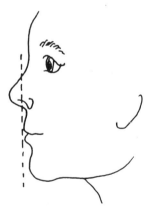

Figure 19   *High Impulsive*   *Low Impulsive*

Those with a high Impulsive trait, tend to interrupt conversations, and may bring up something from out of the blue. They say and do things in the spur of the moment which they later regret. They are inclined to buy impulsively and should ask themselves first whether they really need to purchase a particular item. Before accepting another invitation or taking on another project they need to take a step back and consider their time management. Low impulsive people think before they speak or act. This trait, along with objective thinking, is a quality needed for an executive. They are quick to respond to a situation, but not before giving each situation some considerate thought. Their actions are not ones they regret later.

Trait Combinations

Combine this trait with Credulity (*figure 20*) and a person with these traits may commit themselves to something they may regret later. An example is John McEnroe whose impetuous behavior we have witnessed many times on the tennis court.

Combine Impulsiveness with Objectiveness (*figure 39*) and now you have a very impulsive decision maker. Add the trait of low Acquisitiveness, (this is a person whose ears lay flat against their head, as opposed to protruding, see (*figure 38*) and Risk-Taker to these traits, you now have a formula for a gambler, or someone who has a hard time saving money and is constantly getting into debt. Possible careers for the highly Impulsive are radio, TV, teaching (with low Tolerance), interpreter and sales.

People whose lips recede behind the glabella tend to be more calculated in thought and action. They are more deliberate and not prone to quick or impetuous decisions. People with low Impulsiveness and Sequential Thinking (*figure 40*) will take time to consider a major buying decision. Do not try to rush or pressure these people into making a purchase. Give them some space to think through their decision.

Directing High Impulsiveness

If you are Impulsive, look before you leap or you may regret your decision. Learn not to interrupt a conversation. Pay attention to what is being said, and allow the other person to complete their comment or response. Count to ten before you say anything and leave more of your thoughts unspoken.

Directing Low Impulsiveness

If you are low Impulsive, you may want to consider being more spontaneous, loosen up and go with the spirit of the occasion.

CREDULITY/SKEPTICISM

The physical indicator is the nose viewed from the profile. When the tip of the nose turns upwards, this shows Credulity. This person is more gullible than one with a turned-down nose (indicating Skepticism).

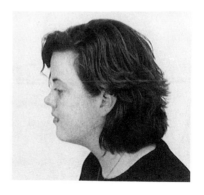

Figure 20   *Credulity*

Gullible people have an instinctive trust in what is told to them. They may find themselves taken advantage of by others and often find themselves falling for other people's practical jokes. They can be naive, and seldom check out credentials, background or authority. On the positive side they are more trusting, open minded, and willing to give new ideas a trial. When considering investments they need to consciously demand proof and get second opinions before committing themselves or their money. Many have fallen under the spell of get rich quick schemes, seldom do you see individuals with the skeptical trait fall for those so called business opportunities.

Skeptical people are less open minded. They automatically doubt or question what is being said, and do not accept things at face value. To some people they may appear distrustful or even hostile. If you need to convince them, make sure you completely satisfy their questions and present them with the facts. Once you have done so, you can win them over. The positive aspect of skepticism is that this person will thoroughly question the reason to buy and not be taken in by those "tall stories."

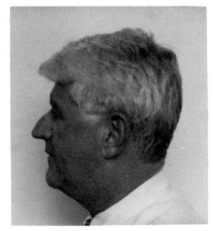

Figure 21   *Skepticism*

Trait Combinations

Combine this trait with Analyticalness, and these people may be considered very opinionated. Well-known examples of the combination are Ross Perot, John Lennon, Bob Hope, Meryl Streep and Steven Spielberg.

Directing Credulity

If you are Credulous, ask more questions when considering a purchase. Do not be taken in by a "good deal". Ask someone who has knowledge about the product or opportunity. A person with high Credulity and Impulsiveness, may find themselves making a purchase or investment they regret later.

Directing Skeptics

When you are dealing with people who are skeptical, remember they have a psychological need for proof or substantiation. When presenting them with a new idea or concept, make sure you present all the important facts. They need facts in order to make up their own minds. To them it appears foolish to accept the facts without getting all the information first. This may appear as a "wet blanket" to others and dampen other people's enthusiasm. Make sure this does not come over as a non-supportive statement in relationships. Get the whole story and all the facts before judging or making up your mind. Try listening to what the other person has to say first, and then ask them if they would like a second opinion. This will avoid misunderstanding or an emotional response of "oh you never think my ideas are any good."

FEELINGS AND EMOTIONS

- Self-Confidence   75
- Tolerance   79
- Self Reproach   84
- Exactingness   85
- Methodicalness   87
- Sharpness   89
- Forward/Backward Balance   91
- Detail Concern   93
- Physical /Mental Motive   95
- Sound and Music Appreciation   97
- Dramatic Appreciation   99
- Emotional Expression   100
- Discrimination   103
- Esthetic Appreciation   106
- Acquisitiveness   108

What lies before us and what lies behind us
are small matters compared to
what lies within us.
And we bring what is within
out into the world,
miracles happen.

- Henry David Thoreau

SELF-CONFIDENCE

The physical indicator is the width of the face at the outside point of the eye brows compared to the length of the face. The more similar the width is to the length of the face the higher the Self-Confidence. If the length of the face is longer compared to the width of the face confidence is built through knowledge. The difference between this trait and Authoritativeness is that the Self-Confident person likes a challenge whereas the Authoritative person (*figure 8*) likes to be in charge.

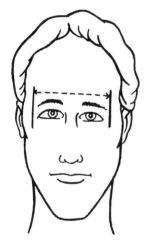

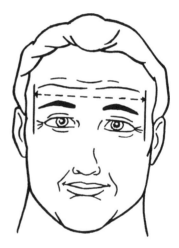

Figure 22 Low Self-Confidence   *High Self-Confidence*

People with high Self-Confidence enjoy a challenge, and focus on results rather than difficulties. If you were to walk into a meeting you could spot them right away, they look in charge. If people with this trait also have high Authoritativeness (*figure 8*) this will add leadership to their qualities. Wearing a suit that is extremely formal adds to their power. Examples are Hillary Clinton, Barbara Bush and Boris Yeltsin.

Women who possess high Self-Confidence need to be careful wearing a strong red suit. Men are not always comfortable with the strength of this message and it may bias feelings before a meeting has begun. However, if this is the woman's intention and she is confident of her position, then enjoy. Assess the situation and make a decision of what to wear based on the business environment and the desired outcome.

High Self-Confidence people are courageous and enjoy life on a large scale. They assume they can tackle anything and will do so with very little hesitation, or concern for confrontations. Because they do not always have all the information to take on the new task at hand, they may fall flat on their face and wonder why. Anne, who has high Self-Confidence admitted she kept taking on some challenging situations not always having the experience or knowledge needed. She felt that with her high level of intelligence there would be no problem. On further discussion there was a realization that she did not always have the necessary information to create a successful outcome. Anne was so caught up with the excitement of launching a new product, that she did not stop to think about her lack of expertise. She felt her ability to handle challenging situations would more than compensate for her lack of experience.

One of the biggest risks for high Self-Confident people is running headlong into each other, especially when in a heated discussion. They will gradually raise their voices in order to be more dominant in the conversation. To individuals who have narrower features (lower Self -Confidence) they appear intimidating because they lead life on a much grander scale. They are very assured people and have natural leadership ability.

Their lesson in life is to learn not to prejudge others with less Self-Confidence. They should not expect them to take on a task outside their expertise until they have all the facts and knowledge to carry out the project. If high Self-Confidence is not handled well, some people, when put into a management position, may become overpowering and intimidating, particularly if they wear strong colors that further amplify their presence. They may expect others to achieve more than is reasonable without prior knowledge. They need to know that it is important to work as a team, rather than as a manager on a throne.

Examples of Trait Combinations

Consider people with high Self-Confidence and high Physical Insulation. These traits could work for or against them. On the reinforcing side, not only are they confident about what they are doing, they do not let situations affect their emotions. For example Clinton has high Self-Confidence traits and high Physical Insulation (*figure 5*) whereas George Bush has lower Self-Confidence and finer hair. If you were to see the two together, without knowing who they were, you would notice that Clinton would appear to be the more confident person of the two. When high Self-Confidence is combined with high Authoritativeness, it creates a take charge person. Examples are Hillary Clinton, The Duchess of York and Boris Yeltsin.

Low Self-Confidence

People with narrower faces can develop a learned Self-Confidence through knowledge and experience. They are very cautious people. By nature they are the support people in a group, and may not necessarily be comfortable in a leadership situation. They are much more aware of what is going on around them and how different situations can affect them and other people. They are more aware of their limitations and stay with what is familiar until they have enough knowledge to take major steps forward.

Individuals who have narrow faces do not carry as much perceived authority as those with wider faces. However, if they have extremely sharp features, are very forceful and competitive they appear to be more Self-Confident in the moment. Their forcefulness takes on a more directed energy.

Take, for example, people with low Self-Confidence, low Physical Insulation (*figure 5*) and take criticism personally. If their work was highly criticized, not only would they internally feel like failures, they would lose what little confidence they had. This is often a situation that occurs in childhood development, when the child does not live up to the expectations of a parent and is constantly criticized. The lesson for those with Low Self-Confidence is not to take criticism too personally and to express to the other person their feelings about the situation.

Low Self-Confident people often undersell themselves. They take off-handed comments personally and if they are also very emotional, they are perceived to over react on small issues. In a public appearance situation they feel ill at ease in the limelight, and are very sensitive to criticism of their presentations. They often doubt their own capabilities. However, once they have gained their knowledge and experience, they have all the confidence in the world. Examples are Julia Roberts, Vanessa Redgrave and Prince William.

Directing High Self-Confidence

If you are highly Self-Confident learn to respect other people's knowledge. Be aware of others while listening to what they are saying. When in a group situation allow others to voice their opinion. Although another person may seem meek and mild they may have something important to contribute. Do not discount them. Be willing to support others through their learning process.

Understand their hesitancy to take on new projects without prior knowledge.

Directing Low Self-Confidence

When asked to take on a new project, find out every thing you need to know. Consult with others who have experience in the related area. Take one step at a time. Let people know what you have accomplished and enjoy the attention. If feelings of low Self-Confidence become a barrier to getting things done, then set out to achieve goals that are obtainable. If the goals cannot be changed, then set a series of milestones so the final goal is reached as a series of smaller accomplishments. Since knowledge and understanding promote confidence, find out all you need to know before launching a project or getting into a new situation. When you find yourself with uncertain feelings, ask whether this is rational, stop and look to see what can be done to change those thought patterns. When working with high Self-Confident people use larger gestures and a stronger tone of voice. If you know beforehand that you will be meeting with individuals who have this trait, select clothing in deeper colors. This will help to support your verbal message.

TOLERANCE

This trait is represented by the distance between the eyes, and determines how much a person will tolerate a situation. When making this measurement, you also need to consider the aperture of the eye. Can a whole eye fit into the space between the two eyes? If so, and there is space left over, then this is a very Tolerant person. If it just fits, then this is a person who is just tolerant. If the space between the eyes is less than an eye width, then this person has very low Tolerance.

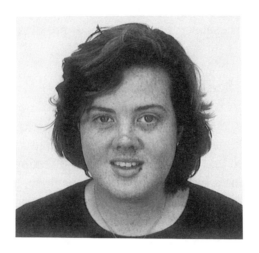

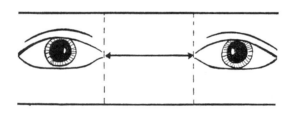

Figure 23   High Tolerance

People with high Tolerance are more permissive, both of themselves and of others. They appear to be very easy going and have a tendency to put things off until tomorrow. Avoiding procrastination is their biggest challenge. They put up with situations too long and need to let others know sooner how they feel otherwise people take advantage of their good nature. They tend to be more relaxed and not to overreact to less tolerant situations. They are more interested in the big picture (macro vision). These people may get easily distracted by what is going on around them and find it hard to stay focused.

When school children have a combination of high Tolerance, low Concentration, short legs and restlessness they may have a short attention span. Until the child and parents have an understanding that this is a part of their genetic make up, these traits in action may be interpreted as disruptive. This could also be an explanation for attention deficit problems. When all parties understand what is going on, the situation can be handled in a much more constructive way. The first step would be to have the child's personology chart made, then discuss the results in a group session with the teacher, parents and child.

High Tolerance individuals are procrastinators, and may find themselves running late for appointments because they want to do just one more thing before they leave their home or office. Their friends and associates may consider them unreliable, when they are really trying to fit in too many activities. Consequently, they over-extend themselves and end up canceling at the last moment, or turning up late for the appointment. Combine this trait with Impetuousness and this could get them into serious trouble. They need to respect other people's time, and if they're going to be late they should call ahead. Think first before accepting all those invitations or volunteering for different causes. Examples of high Tolerance are Hillary Clinton, Brooke Shields, Angela Lansbury and Boris Yeltsin. Although models are probably not picked for their tolerance level, this trait is a dominant characteristic in these people. Next time you look at a magazine, notice how most of them have widely spaced eyes.

Low Tolerance people are much more focused on the issue at hand. They are more interested in the micro picture. They have an intense "now" reaction and have a built-in sense of right and wrong. They like to get it right the first time and are less tolerant of others sloppy workmanship. If they are presented with too many tasks at once they may get frustrated. They are better at handling one job at a time. They get irritated very quickly and do not appreciate being interrupted from what they are doing. They are much more focused on what is happening now. If you want a job done well assign it to low Tolerance person. They will stay focused until the job is completed, unwilling to tolerate interruptions, distractions and poor quality. These people make excellent teachers and supervisors because they do not let situations get out of control. They like a job done well and on schedule. An example of low Tolerance is Barbra Streisand, Monica Seles and John McEnroe.

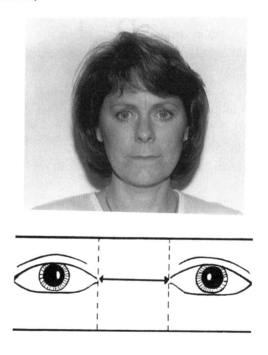

Figure 24   Low Tolerance

Combination Traits

People with fine hair, impatience and low Tolerance will have their tolerance reduced still further. If someone arrives late for an appointment they will be extremely annoyed and consider the visitor to be inconsiderate of their time, whatever the reason. As one individual expressed, "I only select my friends based on their ability to be on time" This individual was totally unforgiving of tardiness. We each need to work on our own traits. Less tolerant people need to slow down their reaction. They need to take time to think before they pass judgment or they may drive others away.

Directing High Tolerance

If you are a high Tolerance person and find yourself working with a low Tolerance person, try not to introduce too many ideas at once - just stay focused on one or two things. When you give the low tolerance person a job to do, you can count on them to stay focused (even though you might not) on what they are doing until it is finished.

Set boundaries and deadlines, and stick to them. Do not put things off until tomorrow. Try not to over commit yourself. Make sure you arrive on time for appointments. If you find yourself running late, call ahead of time to let people know.

Directing Low Tolerance

If you are a low Tolerance person, you may over react without realizing it. Things annoy you, so relax and take a deep breath. Re-focus your thoughts or move away from the situation. Get some exercise or change the thought pattern. Respond rather than react. Do not let minor irritations upset you. Learn to put situations in perspective. Remember your perspective may be different than others.

When working with high Tolerance people, make it known that they need to complete the project on time. Let them know why the project is important, and the consequences of delaying its completion. Create bench marks for them and keep an eye on their progress. If people are late try not to snap at them or pass judgment. Lighten up, this is not the end of the world.

SELF REPROACH

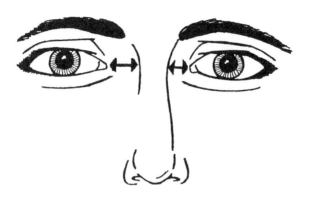

Figure 25   Self -Reproach

Self-Reproach is experienced only when there is a mood swing on tolerance. This trait is indicated when one eye is closer to the bridge of the nose than the other. People with this trait tend to be unpredictable. They feel an inconsistency in their tolerance level. One never knows what to expect. One moment situations do not seem to bother them, then another time they are irritated by every little thing. This may be puzzling to those around them, as they are not sure what to expect. The people themselves never know how they will react. When they react irrationally, whether at work or at home, they are hard on themselves for behaving in such a manner.

Directing Self-Reproach

Understanding your swing in tolerance levels will help you control your reactions. You can control the mood. Remember to think first rather than react. There will be further discussion on mood swings and why they occur. Often times these can be aggravated when an individual is not leading a balanced life. They become irritable for what seems to be little or no reason. Simply taking a walk or engaging in an activity you really enjoy, will help to relieve some of the inner tension.

EXACTINGNESS

The physical indicator is the vertical furrow between the eyebrows and represents the desire for precision. The longer the furrow the higher the score. This physical trait is developed (rather than inherited) by repeated muscular tension from prolonged concentration.

People who score high on Exactingness are concerned with the information being exact, precise and accurate. They like to check and recheck everything they do until they are convinced everything is correct. They may be considered too fussy and nit-picking by others when a situation does not need such scrutiny.

Possible vocations that demand exactingness and tend to develop this trait are proof-reading, auditing, computer programming, accounting, investigating, diamond cutting, and dental work.

Figure 26   Exactingness

85

Trait Combinations
When this trait is combined with high Tolerance (*figure 23*) a person has to put a greater emphasis on focusing and getting things exactly right. This is often seen in actors and actresses. This may be due to the demands made of them during their work.

Directing Exactingness
If you are an exacting person, try to relax when working on projects. Recognize when you are fussing over unimportant or irrelevant details. Don't get stuck on the details, focus more on the results. If you must delegate a task to someone else, keep in mind details may not have the same level of importance to them. Be more flexible if importance for the task at hand is not a priority.

Directing Low Exactingness
People who score low on this trait need to take particular care to re-check everything before giving the project their final approval. Take responsibility for the end results.

METHODICALNESS

The physical expression of Methodicalness is observed directly above the eyebrows where a muscle has developed a ridge across the forehead. The trait is developed through intense concentration on a methodical process. This can become an obsession. It may start out as Exactingness (*figure 26*) and then progress to Detail concern finally developing into Methodicalness.

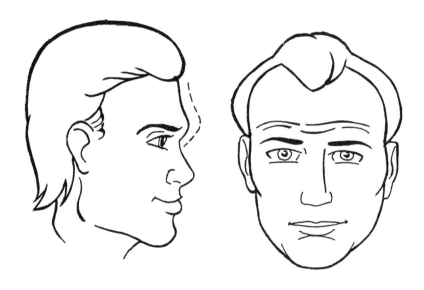

Figure 27 High Methodicalness.   Overly concerned with details.

People with this trait like to complete each step before moving on. This is their routine way of doing things. They are not adaptable and become stuck in a rut because of the pattern they fall into. Being so methodical may take the spontaneity out of relationships. The responses, actions and approaches become so predictable that after a while it will appear boring to the other people. Try to break the patterns now and again to keep interest and intrigue going. Methodical individuals like to have everything worked out beforehand, something which irritates people who need to have a project completed in a shorter time. Careers and hobbies which demand a meticulous step by step process develop this trait.

Figure 28 High Methodicalness.

Trait Combinations

People with Methodicalness and Subjective Thinking (*figure 40*) have an even slower thinking process. These people cannot be hurried, either in filling out forms or starting new projects. If you do have a time commitment, ask if there is anything you can do to speed up the process.

Directing Methodicalness

If you are a methodical person, make a conscious effort to be more adaptable. Do not impose your routine on others. Deliberately re-arrange your routine from time to time, to get in touch with your more creative side.

Directing Low Methodicalness

Recognize the benefits of doing tasks in a step by step process. It may seem boring to you, however, the outcome may be well worth the effort when a methodical process is used.

SHARPNESS

This trait is decided by the sharpness (angularity) of the facial features as seen from the profile. People who have sharp profile features are very aware of what is going on around them. They have a sense of what is happening without being told, and enjoy ferreting out information. They pay attention to detail which would be an asset in a career such as accounting or finance. A head hunter expressed his frustration of trying to find someone who was more detail oriented. He would hire people who stated they were very detailed only to discover this was not the case. Upon consulting with the author of this book, his problem was resolved. It has been observed that when an individual's skin is very tight across the bone structure and they also have sharp features, there is a tendency to be very fussy. Their homes or offices would look clinically clean. These individuals are often seen in careers such as dental hygienist and nutrition.

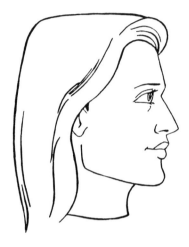

Figure 29   Sharpness

Trait Combinations

When this trait is combined with Objectiveness (*figure 39*), Forward Balance, Impatience, and Low Tolerance (*figure 23*) this is likely to produce quick responses. A good example of this trait combination in action was the Prosecuting attorney for the O.J. Simpson case, Marcia Clark. She is well known for her success in winning criminal cases. Other examples are Meryl Streep, Margaret Thatcher and Prince Philip.

Careers for this combination could be accounting, law, investigation, quality control, inspection, FBI agent and dietitian.

FORWARD/BACKWARD BALANCE

This trait is shown by how much face is appearing in front of the ear in comparison to the amount behind the ear towards the back of the head. This is best seen from the side view. When there is more face in front, this is known as Forward Balance.

People with Forward Balance think in terms of the present and the future. There is a strong need for recognition and appreciation. They enjoy being on stage whether it is giving a presentation, teaching or in the theater. They need praise and acknowledgment. To others they may be perceived as "stealing the show". They need to allow others the opportunity for recognition and contribution. These people are less considerate of others. This trait is seen in many juvenile offenders. They enjoy the spotlight and recognition that comes from their peer group. Once their traits have been positively directed, they may well become upstanding members in the community.

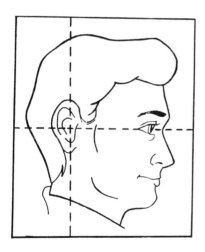

Figure 30 Forward Balance

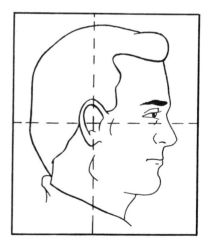

Backward Balance

Backward Balance is shown by how far forward the ear is set on the face. People with Backward Balance relate to what has historically happened and live in the present. They rely on past experiences and accomplishment. It is harder for them to plan long term projects. Although people who score high on Backward Balance are more considerate, they have a tendency to hold grudges over a long period of time. They enjoy working in the background and have a harder time selling themselves.

They are less concerned with what others think and more interested in what they are doing. They are not very concerned themselves about recognition. At the same time they may resent being overlooked.

Careers for Forward Balance could be radio commentator, model, master of ceremonies, actor/actress, racing, teaching. Careers for Backward Balance could be historian, genealogist, librarian, history teacher.

Directing Forward Balance

If you have Forward Balance, remember to include others in the spotlight. Remember that not everyone wants to move at your pace. Take classes in the theater. Teach workshops. When working with others who are Backward Balance, direct the conversation so that the results you want will be achieved. For example, if the person you are working with fails to see the need for long term planning, explain to them the benefits gained by mapping out the future for business or family activities.

Directing Backward Balance

If you have Backward Balance, learn to let go of what has happened, it's "water under the bridge". Do not bore others with your repeated conversation of what others have done to you. Forgive and forget. Blow your own trumpet, let other people know what you are doing and accomplishing. Take advantage of new opportunities.

DETAIL CONCERN

This trait is indicated by the noticeable development of small mounds above each side of the inner eyebrow. It indicates that a person is constantly paying attention to detail. This trait is developed through work or creative activity, rather than inherited. It is common in computer programmers, dentists, accountants, diamond cutters, surgeons and anyone working with fine detail and precision. People who score high on this trait may become obsessed by detail. They will find themselves checking and re-checking to make sure everything is in order. Their co-workers and family might find this frustrating, because at times it interferes with a job being completed.

Suitable careers for people who have Detail Concern would be accounting, editing, drafting, computer design and all areas of safety or health.

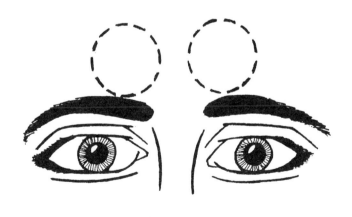

Figure 31   *Detail Concern*

93

Directing High Detail Concern
If you are over concerned with detail, keep it in perspective and ignore it when it is not important. Do not impose your concern for detail on family or relationships.

Directing Low Detail Concern
When Detail Concern is important to another person, make the extra effort and pay attention to details even though they are unimportant to you. Recognize other people's need for precision and make the extra effort to re-check your work. In the long run this will save time, money and avoid conflicts generated by sloppy work.

PHYSICAL/MENTAL MOTIVE

The indicator for Physical and Mental Motive is the length from the base of the chin to the base of the nose in comparison to the length of the face. When this feature appears to be longer a person responds physically to situations, rather than mentally. If it is shorter a person will think through the situation first before responding. There is the saying "a person moves the piano first rather than moving the stool". This would indicate the physical response. While the reaction of the individual with the opposite trait would say, "let's think about this first" before they act on the situation.

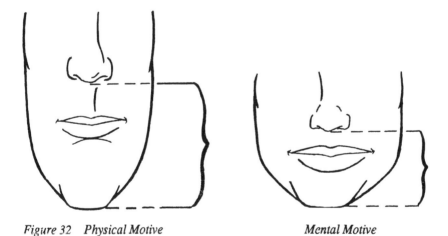

Figure 32   Physical Motive   *Mental Motive*

People who score high on Physical Motive like to be where the action is, and to be physically active. It is harder for them to slow down and relax. They have so much energy that sometimes they do not know what to do with themselves. Without high physical activity they quickly become bored and restless. It is hard for them to sit still for long periods of time. When Physical Motive is combined with high Foot Dexterity (*figure 1*) this amplifies the need for high physical activity. People who have a lower need for physical outlet may find it harder to keep up with them. In relationships the physical person will be more demanding in their sexual drive and may feel frustrated when their partner does not respond with the same intensity or need. Children who score high on this trait have boundless energy. This energy needs to be channeled into activities such as soccer, tennis or gymnastics. Many sports players are extremely physical people, for example Joe Montana, Jimmy Connors, Boris Becker, Chris Everet and Steffi Graff.

People who score high on Mental Motive (the space is shorter from the base of the chin to the base of the nose) are stimulated by mental challenges. Mental activity is as consuming to them as physical activity is to the physically motivated. They accomplish more through the mental process than through physical action. Without a mental challenge they may become bored in their jobs. It takes them a longer period of time to recover from high physical activity. Their physical side may be neglected because of their strong desire for mental activity. Just as the physical person needs to take time out to use their mind, so does the mentally motivated person need to take time out for exercise. Examples are Richard Gere, Meryl Streep and Steven Spielberg.

Directing Physical Motive

People who are more Physically Motivated need to strike a balance of rest and exercise. Others who score low on this trait will find it difficult to keep up the same pace. When reacting to a situation, slow your physical response down and think first before acting.

Directing Mental Motive

Balance your mental activity with physical needs. Make sure you set time aside for physical exercise. When you are involved with high physical activity for long periods, make sure you take time out to rest.

SOUND AND MUSIC APPRECIATION

This trait is indicated by the outer helix and inner rim of the ear. When the outer edge is curved without any notch, the appreciation of music is high. If the inner rim is also completely round without the slightest notch, this indicates pitch and the ability to play a musical instrument. This trait also indicates a high sense of rhythm and flow. When individuals with this trait engage in activities with their hands such as, working at the potters wheel or giving a massage, they experience a deep sense of rhythm and connection which gives them a deep satisfaction.

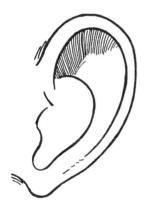
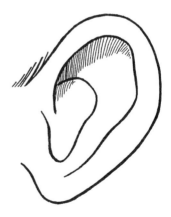

Figure 33   Music Appreciation   *Low Pitch Ability*

When Musical Appreciation is combined with fine hair and Esthetic Appreciation (*figure 37*) this person will have a heightened sensitivity and appreciation of music. Next time you see a musical group, notice the roundness of the outer and inner edges of the ear. You will find that most musicians will have this trait along with high Esthetic Appreciation. An example is Luciano Pavarotti.

Children who have low pitch ability struggle for years to master an instrument with limited success. Yet their parents insist they continue with the music lessons, not realizing that this is not a natural activity for their child. People who have a high music appreciation love to attend concerts and listen to music for the greater part of the day. The first thing they do when getting into a car is turn on the radio. People with Music Appreciation and fine hair tend to keep the music low key. However, when this trait is combined with coarse hair, they are more likely to turn up the volume.

Directing Low Music Appreciation

Do not insist that the child has to take music lessons. Let them make the decision. Consider another activity the child will really enjoy. We are not all born to become Mozart or Pavarotti. A possible alternative could be percussion instruments where the emphasis is on rhythm rather than pitch.

Directing High Music Appreciation

Children who have this innate ability should be encouraged to take music lessons. Teenagers could form a musical group. An ideal gift for an individual with high musical appreciation would be tickets to a concert series.

DRAMATIC APPRECIATION

Dramatic Appreciation is indicated by how much the eyebrow rises above the orbital bone (top of the eye socket). Examples are Doctor Spock, Boris Yeltsin, Elizabeth Taylor, Lena Horn and Cher. When you look at them face on you will notice the eyebrows go upwards in a very dramatic sweep. This is an advantage for those individuals who are in the theater. This trait is mostly seen in woman.

Figure 34   Dramatic Appreciation

People with Dramatic Appreciation exaggerate both verbally and physically when expressing themselves. They over dramatize their feelings and emotions especially when this trait is combined with forward balance and high emotionality. At times they appear overly theatrical and less sincere. People who have this trait with Verboseness (*figure 18*) make good story tellers.

Their dramatic flare shows in their style of dress and the interior design of their home and office. People who have high Dramatic Appreciation are at home in the theater, teaching seminars or in any situation where they have a captive audience.

Directing Dramatic Appreciation

The dramatic person's challenge is to know when to keep things simple, stay with the facts and not dramatically embellish. Use this talent for presentations or the theater. Keep the drama in check, and use when needed to emphasize a point or situation. Take classes in acting at the local college or join an amateur dramatic group. Share the limelight with others, know when it is appropriate to take a back seat and be the audience.

EMOTIONAL EXPRESSION

Emotional Expression is found by the size of the iris in relationship to the sclera (white of the eye). The larger the iris, the greater is the amount of emotion that is outwardly expressed. People with a high score are more likely to show and express what they feel to a greater degree. They are more affectionate and display more warmth and feelings whether showing sorrow, happiness or enthusiasm. In a relationship they expect the same emotional need. They express their feelings more openly. At times they are extreme in their emotional expression, especially when this trait is combined with low tolerance and dramatic appreciation. When their emotions are running very high they need to be aware that the situation can be completely blown out of context. Others who do not have this trait will be puzzled by this extreme behavior.

People who score low on Emotional Expression are able to deal more dispassionately with others. They make decisions with their head rather than the heart. Their eyes are less expressive, and run the risk of appearing indifferent, cold or unemotional. They feel as deeply as an emotionally expressive person, but they keep their feelings hidden under the surface. Low Emotional Expressive people are not as outwardly affectionate and find it difficult to express what they feel. They stay outwardly calm and work well in situations where emotions are getting out of control. They pride themselves on their emotional control.

Figure 35   High Emotional Expression   *Low Emotional Expression*

Trait Combinations

When Emotional Expression is combined with fine hair, feelings are amplified. People with this trait combination may intensely feel other people's sadness, although they may not personally know the people involved in the tragedy. They are greatly moved by what is happening around them. Because their emotions are more obvious, it doesn't necessarily mean that their inner feelings are any stronger than those of a person who is less emotionally expressive. They find themselves "wrapped up" in their emotions, and the situation may get out of perspective.

Directing Low Emotional Expression

People with low expressiveness will benefit by showing their affections more openly, and letting others know how they feel. When the feelings are not revealed by facial expression it is perfectly acceptable to use words.

Directing High Emotional Expression

Women who have high emotional expression may be perceived by men as flirtatious and inviting sexual advancement. This can be avoided with body language, physical distancing and toning down the emotional level of communication. If you have low tolerance, fine hair and are high emotional, try to keep your reactions under control, or others around you will think you are over reacting and be turned off by your behavior.

In a sales situation, where the customers are more emotionally expressive, interact with high emotional people on their emotional level. Notice the amount of expression in their eyes, this will tell you how the sale or presentation is progressing.

DISCRIMINATION

Discrimination is the compulsion to be more selective. It is measured by the distance from the top rim of the eyelid to the base of the brow. The greater the distance between the two, the more discriminating or selective the person. Discriminating people appear more formal, reserved and less approachable. Others who are more affable, may consider these people to be snobbish and less accessible. During a sales presentation you may hear them say "I would like to think about this for a while." Recognize where that person is coming from and give them the space they need to make their decision.

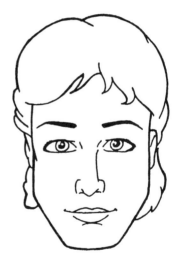

Figure 36   *Affableness*   *Discrimination*

A person who is more discriminating will take time to consider all aspects of a situation before making a commitment, whether it is the friends they have around them, the purchases they make, or other life situations. Do not try to rush these people into a decision. They need more time to consider if this is something they really want to do. Examples are Margaret Thatcher and Boris Yeltsin.

Less discriminating people are more affable, less selective in the people they have around them, and the products they purchase. They are more informal in their general approach and style and appear to be very amiable. They establish an immediate rapport and make friends easily. They are more laid back in their approach and move in on situations quickly. Often times they will touch people on the arm or give them a spontaneous hug. This trait is more dominant in men which partly explains their need to make physical contact. Many say they hold back from immediate contact for fear of misinterpretation. Examples are Andre Agassi and Richard Gere.

Individuals who are more discriminating and have careers or activities such as massage, chiropractor or any activity with hands on contact, tend to be more spontaneous in their physical contact.

Trait Combinations

Combine low Discrimination with Impetuousness and high Emotional Expression and the effect will be amplified. People who have this trait combination may jump into a partnership that they may regret later. This is often seen in early marriages, where decisions are made based on strong emotional feelings. Taking a moment to think first before making that all important commitment may make the difference between a good decision or one which could end up out of control.

Directing Affableness

When less discriminating (affable) people interact with those who are more discriminating they need to remember not to become too familiar and casual. Let the discriminating person make the first step. Do not be over friendly or they will initially retreat. Ask "permission" before entering their space. When in their home do not invade their space (see ten-acre principle). Be more formal on first contact with high Discrimination people. Do not make physical contact unless you really know them. Be more selective when choosing friends or making a purchase.

Directing Discrimination

If you are Discriminating, quickly put others at ease. Practice being more friendly. Colors you wear create formal or informal messages. When you want to appear more approachable wear softer colors.

ESTHETIC APPRECIATION

High Esthetic Appreciation is shown when the eyebrows form a straight line that extends beyond the outer corner of the eye. This shows the need for environmental balance, emotional balance, harmony and appreciation of the esthetics.

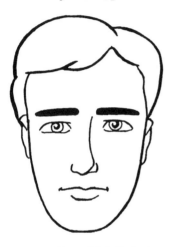

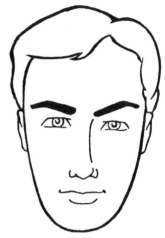

Figure 37   *High Esthetic*   *Low Esthetic*

Balance and harmony are extremely important for people with high Esthetic Appreciation. When they feel upset they will rarely raise their voices or make "emotional waves." They will do anything to create balance and harmony in their lives. When there is a lack of harmony they may seek drugs or alcohol to dull the discord. Teenagers and adults who are highly esthetic fall victim to substance abuse when their home environment is out of balance; it is a way of escape. They drink for the feeling it gives them, despite the outcome. They seek to lose themselves, rather than identify and deal with what is real. Until they are willing to take responsibility, they are prisoners of their own senses. They need to look at the reason their lives are out of balance. Otherwise the situation may get out of hand.

High Esthetics are often passionately interested in art, music and photography. They have a fine sense of balance and harmony and quickly notice when things around them are not right.

People who have low Esthetic Appreciation are not so affected by their surroundings, they are able to cope better.

Directing Esthetic Appreciation

Be responsible for yourself and learn to take charge. Do not get caught up in a situation where the activity is controlling your life. Get in touch with yourself through Yoga, Tai Chi, meditation classes or walking. Take up a hobby that is an extension of your personal expression.

This trait is seen in many models, musicians and artists. Examples are Elvis Presley, Brooke Shields, Dustin Hoffman, Newt Gingrich and John Major.

ACQUISITIVENESS

Acquisitiveness is determined by how much of the ear lobe can be seen when looking at a person face on. The more it is exposed, the higher is the score. As the lobe starts to lay flat against the head, the lower the score. People who score high on Acquisitiveness and Conservation (*figure 41*) are the "pack rats". They love to collect things and are very possessive of what they acquire, and seldom dispose of things. They enjoy playing the stock market.

Figure 38   High Acquisitiveness   *Low Acquisitiveness*

They appear very selfish, and have a hard time parting with their possessions or money. They put their possessions first before family or friends. This trait is amplified when they also score high on Administrativeness (*figure 17*) and Conservation (*figure 41*). At a young age they should be encouraged to start a savings account. Examples of Acquisitiveness are Prince Charles, his sons and Ross Perot.

Less acquisitive people are inclined to discard possessions, and avoid saving for the future. When this trait is combined with construction (*figure 41*) they enjoy throwing things out, and have a detachment from their possessions when they are no longer useful. This may be a problem if the low Acquisitive person volunteers to help others sort out their belongings. They may well discard items before checking with the owner first. If you solicit their help, make sure they check with you first before they throw something out which is perceived as valuable to you. If they are out shopping and have ten dollars left in their pockets they will spend it on something, although the item is not needed. Money flows through their fingers and they often waste it on impulse buying. These people need to take classes on investments, financial planning or get professional assistance to protect their money. If one side of the face is high on Acquisitiveness and the other side low there will be swing moods between saving and splurging.

Hobbies are collections of any kind, such as stamps, rocks, dolls, coins and games that involve purchasing or acquiring property.

Careers that interest highly Acquisitive people are import/export, stock broker, real estate and banking.

Trait Combinations

High Acquisitiveness and Administrativeness people are good with investments. They will always look for a good bargain. People with a combination of low Acquisitiveness, Automatic Giving (*figure 13*), Impetuousness and Considerateness will give away their last penny. Real Estate agents have a trait combination of Conservation (*figure 41*) and Acquisitiveness. This indicates their interest in acquiring property and remodeling.

Directing High Acquisitiveness

If you are an acquisitive person, learn to share with others. Study investments. Remember you can enjoy your life today and still plan for tomorrow. When this trait is seen in children, encourage them to have a savings account. Talk to them about the importance of investments and how the stock market works.

Directing Low Acquisitiveness

Take a class on investments. Discipline yourself to put aside some money each month. Buy only what you need. Do not give away or throw out other people's possessions. They may place a very high value on them, whether sentiment or price.

*Each of us is meant to have a character all our own,
to be what no other can exactly be,
and do what no other can exactly do.*

- William Ellery Channing

THINKING TRAITS

- Objective/Subjective   115

- Construction/Conservation   119

- Analytical   121

- Critical Perception   124

- Judgment Variation   126

- Rhetoric   128

When you are insprired by some great purpose,
some extraordinary project, all your thoughts break their bounds:
Your mind transcends limitations,
your consciousness expands in every direction
and you find yourself in a new,
great and wonderful world.

Dormant forces,
facilities and talents become alive,
and you discover yourself to be a greater person
by far than you ever dreamed yourself to be.

- Patanjali

OBJECTIVE/SUBJECTIVE

This trait is located at the front of the forehead, and is best viewed from the side profile. When the forehead is more vertical (upright), a person is more Subjective (Sequential) in their thinking process, whereas a forehead that slopes back at an angle is more Objective, quicker to respond in the moment. This does not describe intelligence, but the speed at which a person responds, processes information or reacts.

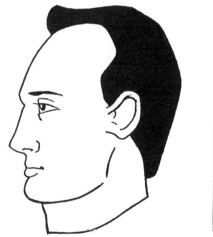 

Figure 39   Objective Thinking

People who have a forehead that slopes back at an angle are more Objective. They jump quickly to conclusions and second guess what other people are going to say or do. They respond quickly to what is happening around them and react well to emergencies. This trait is an asset in sports where quick reactions are needed, such as tennis at the net, ice hockey, car racing or volley ball. Objective people lack sequentially, they do not evaluate enough. They quickly jump to conclusions without getting all the information. When people score high on Objectiveness, they want quick results and appear impatient when others around them move at a slower pace. In contrast Subjective people often seem slow because they are more theoretical and reflective in their thinking. Sometimes, they start a conversation in the middle of a sentence. They are so clear in their head about what they are thinking, they forget the other person may not have a clue about what is being said, this can cause confusion. As children, they have been known to play with mythical characters. When working with children who are Subjective, recognize they may need repetition in order to understand their work. Once this study pattern is established, they can do well in school. A successful program was developed in Hawaii by the late Elizabeth Whiteside who counseled subjective thinking children, who may have otherwise been classified as slow learners.

Subjective thinkers go through a sequential process and use acquired knowledge more constructively. They need time to assimilate information. There is a tendency to blank out when learning under pressure. This may be a problem when taking exams. They need to prepare for tests several days beforehand, whereas Objective students like to cram at the last moment. People who are more sequential need to think through situations and do not like to be rushed. When a teacher goes too fast, the Sequential people are left behind. They are overwhelmed by the rapid delivery and if they miss a step of the process, they become confused and shut down. Their inner conversation is that they're not as smart as the others because they can't keep up and get left behind. However, once the piece of the puzzle is in place, the process becomes very clear. They need to give themselves plenty of time to review their work. Once the Subjective Thinking trait has been identified, both the student and the teacher can work more effectively together. This trait has been observed to be more dominant in females.

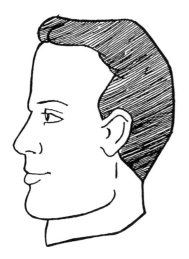 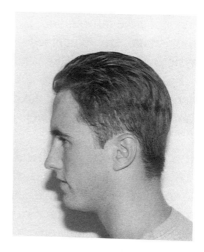

Figure 40   Subjective Thinking

Sequential people are slower in their reactions to practical daily life situations. When they feel pressured, and others request them to speed up, it becomes overwhelming. If they are being pressured into buying within a restricted time frame they may purchase nothing. They like to be sure of their purchasing decision first. When this trait is combined with an action trait such as high

Physicalness or any other action trait like low analytical, it will shorten the response time.

An example of a Subjective person is Ronald Reagan. Examples of Objective people are General Colin Powell, Ed Bradley and Margaret Thatcher.

Trait Combinations

Combine Subjective Thinking with low Self-Confidence and backward balance, these people will take longer to launch a new concept or product. However, once they have accumulated and understood the information, there is no hesitation, particularly when these traits are combined with high action traits such as Physicalness.

Possible careers for Objective people are airline pilot, emergency service, tennis, basketball, control tower operator, radio announcer, car and motorcycle racing.

Directing Objective Thinking

If you are an Objective person, do not jump to conclusions. The temptation is to move ahead. Take time to listen and read through the material rather than skimming the surface. The Objective people handle emergencies well. However, in the slower pace of daily life and work, they will benefit by taking more time to think things through, rather than jumping to conclusions.

Directing Subjective Thinking

If you are a Subjective thinker, prepare well before getting into new situations. When you feel pressured into an immediate decision, create a step by step plan systematically. This exercise will help alleviate the pressure. In a sales situation, do not try to pressure these people or they will leave without buying. Subjective people need to speed up the pace when working with those who are more Objective and when deadlines are immediate.

CONSTRUCTION and CONSERVATION

This trait describes how a person thinks, either outward (construction) towards challenge and new projects or inward (conservation) towards maintenance and preservation.

 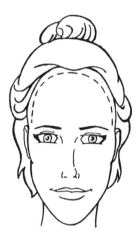

Figure 41   *Construction*   *Conservation*

The physical indicator is the squareness or roundness on the outside edge of the forehead above the temples as seen from the front. An example of the Construction forehead is Ross Perot. Jimmy Carter is a good example of the more rounded, Conservation forehead.

The person with a square forehead enjoys starting new projects, and in extreme cases does not complete or maintain them because of eagerness to start yet another project. The people who score high on construction like to work with new concepts. Their work

119

becomes their hobby. Repetitious assignments quickly bore them. Once a project is completed, they want to move on to something new and challenging. They do not like to patch or repair, and prefer to tear down and start afresh. They like new ideas (replacing old ones), research, pioneering, new tools and materials.

Construction people are more interested in a career rather than working in the home. This sometimes causes a conflict with marital relationships. The husband prefers his wife to stay at home (or vice versa) and look after the children whereas the wife feels frustrated because her strong desire to have a job is not being fulfilled. People with a high Construction trait need to take an outside job or work out of the home to live a balanced life. They need a purpose to their day. Work becomes a hobby for them and others may perceive them as workaholics. They need to be reminded to play once in a while. Once focused, they find themselves lost in their thoughts for long periods of time. Careers include Research, construction, architecture and engineering.

People with a high Conservation trait like to preserve what they have, and enjoy the comforts of home. The family and home are extremely important to them. They are the maintainers and nurturers and enjoy fixing up old things such as homes, furniture refinishing and renovating old cars. They are pack rats, inclined to hang on to everything in case it could be of value or use some day. They often have a very short attention span and they appear impatient during discussions of new ideas or concepts. People with high Conservation do not like waste or spoilage, whereas the Construction person likes to start afresh rather than use what is at hand. Examples of Conservation are Bill Clinton and Princess Margaret.

Trait Combinations

When a person scores high on Construction and Physicalness (*figure 7*) this indicates a strong driving force to initiate new projects. If High Tolerance is added to the previous traits, the individual may take on too many projects. Both the energy and focus will be less effective.

People with High Conservation and Growing Trend, are interested in environmental issues. They enjoy participating and leading workshops on personal growth. When those two traits are also combined with Sharp features they are likely to be interested in nutrition and natural health foods.

Directing Construction

If you score high on construction, learn to make do with what is available. Don't be so hasty in discarding materials that could be used another day. Remember to put your family first.

Directing Conservation

If you are a person who scores high on Conservation, be more open to starting new projects or considering new ideas. Periodically go through your possessions, donate or throw out items you really have no use for. When you find yourself getting impatient, take time out to think before reacting.

Careers include interior design, nursing, dentistry (with high hand coordination), catering, hotel operations, project manager, environmental studies, medicine, chemistry, social services and politics.

ANALYTICAL

The analytical trait is determined by how much or how little of the eyelid is exposed. The more the eyelid is covered by the fold of the skin, the higher is the Analytical score. This person needs to know the reasons behind a situation. When the eyelid is more exposed, this person is less Analytical and more action driven.

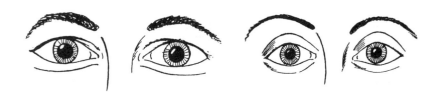

Figure 42   High Analytical   *Low Analytical*

Analytical people need to look into all aspects of a situation or new purchase before entering into it. They like to ferret out information, and will not act before they have all the information needed to make a decision. They love to take things apart and figure out how they work. Combining the Analytical trait with Skepticism (*figure 21*) increases the need to gather further information before accepting a new concept or product. When making a new purchase, they will research and compare quality, performance and price. They enjoy analytical games, researching and analyzing information. Analytical people with sharp features may be viewed by others as extremely picky, e.g., Meryl Streep. These people make good investigators or FBI agents. Other examples of highly Analytical people are Paul Newman, Richard Gere and Princess Diana.

People who are less Analytical prefer to act right away without asking too many questions. Long drawn-out explanations are boring to them. They are more matter of fact and to the point. Low Analytical people are sometimes considered ruthless because they like to get to the core of things quickly, ignoring the subtleties and different facets which others have meticulously researched for them. They like to cut through the red tape and get things accomplished. Once they understand the concept they will want to take action or get directly to the point. In order to do this, they will cut people off in the middle of their conversation. Others will find this action rather rude, and feel what they had to say was of little importance to that person.

Trait Combinations
When a low Analytical trait is combined with low Emotionality and Inconsiderateness, this affect can be amplified to the point of unkindness. However, choice always supercedes structure.

Directing High Analyticalness
If you are highly Analytical, spend less time analyzing when it is not necessary. Speed up the process. Understand that others do not feel the need to know everything and get to the point quickly.

Directing Low Analyticalness
If you are not an Analytical person, then understand others may need to know more pertinent information. Slow down your reaction time. Be prepared to explain, in detail, information to people who are more analytical. Honor their need to know. In a selling situation this will create a feeling of trust. When you ask high Analytical people to take on a task, they may bombard you with questions. They have a compulsion to know more about your request. Try not to cut them off in mid-sentence unless there are time restraints. Communication of time restraints will avoid hurt feelings.

CRITICAL PERCEPTION

Critical Perception is represented by the lower outer edge of the eye. If the outer edge is lower than the inner corner, this is an indicator of someone who is very critical. An example is O. J. Simpson. Notice how the outer part of the eye is lower. When both the inner and outer edges of the eye are either level or begin to slant upwards this shows the person is less critical.

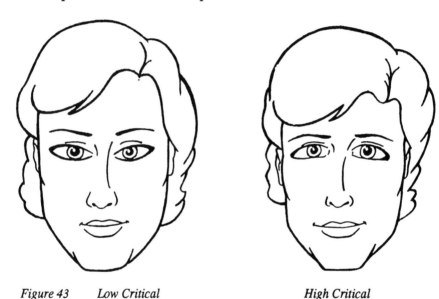

Figure 43   *Low Critical*   *High Critical*

The first thing a critical person sees is what's wrong. Their focus goes directly to that which varies from their expected norm, whether it is a project or behavior. They become very irritated by sloppy workmanship. It is an *automatic* thought process. For some people this is extremely annoying especially in the family environment and relationships. However, this built in attitude is invaluable for the inspection of newly manufactured jet aircraft engines, which hundreds of lives will depend on.

Individuals who have fine hair and a short upper lip do not handle criticism well, their feelings get hurt very quickly. You may feel they over react because it is not your intention to hurt their feelings. When giving criticism to these people first acknowledge their accomplishments and efforts. Point out what could be improved if your advice is requested.

When the eyes slant upwards at the outer corners, these individuals may miss details that are important to safety, calculations or documentation. They first notice what has been achieved rather than what is wrong. They are non-critical people. Other traits such as Sharpness, Low Tolerance and Analyticalness would heighten the low Critical person's awareness of imperfections in a product.

Trait Combinations

People with a combination of high Criticalness, high Physical Insulation (*figure 5*), Low Considerateness or Low Tolerance (*figure 24*) will be extremely critical without consideration for other peoples' feelings. Their reaction will be shorter due to their low tolerance. These people can be very difficult to please. However, once aware of these traits, they can re-direct them more effectively. As one person put it, she turns off the trait when it's not needed.

When there are trait combinations of Critical Perception and Analyticalness (*figure 42*) the effect is amplified. This can result in uncalled-for critique that may hurt the feelings of people who see no need to be digging up faults and problems. It can also prove to be difficult when recognition and achievement of a project are more important than how well the project has been done. Critical people make good critics (obviously) for books, films, art and business situations, particularly where an Analytical capability can add insight and perspective.

Directing High Critical Perception

If you are a Critical person, use criticism for on the job situations. Learn to use it in a constructive way. Remember to give equal amounts of praise and acknowledgment when the job is well done. To criticize fellow workers too much may be counter-productive and result in hard feelings. If you are a parent who has this trait, try not to critique your child's work. Praise him/her for what they have done. If you notice something wrong, that could effect a project, gently ask if there is anything they would like to change.

Directing Low Critical Perception

If you are less Critical be more aware of flaws on the job. Get a second opinion from those who score high in Criticalness. Double check to make sure you have not overlooked an important fact.

JUDGMENT VARIATION

Judgment Variation is indicated when one eye is higher than the other. Notice in Figure 44 both the right and left inner canthi (inner corners of eye) of the eye. Are they level with each other, or is one slightly higher or significantly higher? When it is noticeably higher, people tend to have unconventional judgment and experience changeable mood swings. At times the mood change will cause confusion to those around them. They need to think on the situation before changing their action. At times their judgment is very different from those around them. They will come up with less conventional ways of solving a problem. To those who are more conservative, some of these extreme approaches will be uncomfortable. The unconventional person will approach new designs or ways to solve problems with a different perspective, whether designing a new building, creating an advertisement or a theatrical production.

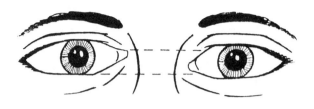

Figure 44   Judgment Variation

The person with both eyes level will be more conventional and accepting of the standards set by society.   They are more predictable and conservative in their approach.   Unconventional approaches and behavior are uncomfortable for them.

Directing Judgment Variation

If you have High Judgment Variation, then this trait can work for or against you.   Use unconventional approaches when it's beneficial, otherwise be open to using conventional methods.   When you are experiencing mood changes, that could effect decisions and current activities, take time out and give your actions more thought.

Directing Low Judgment Variation

If you have low Judgment Variation, be willing to adapt to less conventional ideas when appropriate.

RHETORIC

This trait is shown by the lines under each eye that goes from the inner corner of the eye and continue toward the outer corner. The more lines and the greater length, the higher is the score. People with a strong Rhetoric trait have gift for words and love to use a large vocabulary.

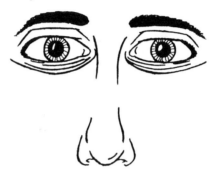

Figure 45   Rhetoric

They enjoy looking up the meanings of words, their origins and derivatives. They have a great appreciation of effective and elegant use of the language. Clumsy and incorrect word usage is offensive to them, particularly by people in high positions. When this trait is combined with Analyticalness (*figure 42*) they are particularly insistent about word usage, and are quick to correct others who use grammar and words incorrectly.

Possible careers for people who score high on this trait are writing, journalism, technical writer, editing, poetry and teaching.

Directing High Rhetoric

Listen to the content of what is being said, rather than interrupt a person's conversation for incorrect word usage.

Directing Low Rhetoric

Build up your vocabulary daily by looking up a word in the dictionary that you have heard or read that day. Then write down several different sentences using that word. Take a creative writing class to expand your word usage.

FAMOUS FACES

GÉRARD DEPARDIEU

Gérard Depardieu is a very friendly individual with an insatiable curiosity for news and information. This is shown by the roundness of the nose and flat forehead. Because he likes to start new projects, he may find himself not completing or maintaining previous ones. Ideas are constantly milling around in his head and when he decides to do something there is no stopping him. His protruding chin shows he has a tremendous amount of tenacity. His analytical eyes tell us he takes his work seriously, and asks many questions before making a decision. Balance and harmony are important to his life. He may enjoy collecting old works of art and photography, and probably has a wonderful collection of books. He will respond physically to an emergency and needs to remember to act rather than react. Competitive sports would be a good outlet for his physical and combative spirit. He is at home with nature and likes to contribute to the quality of other people's lives.

HILLARY CLINTON

The width of Hillary Clinton's face shows an extremely self-confident and authoritative person. She likes to take on a challenge and enjoys the recognition that goes along with her job. Her curved eyebrows show she is an excellent program coordinator and has good organization skills. Her wide set eyes say she is a very tolerant person and tends to procrastinate. Her challenge is to stay focused. As a long-term planner, she will get irritated by those who move at a slower pace. Her large lower lip shows she is generous with her time and enjoys maintaining projects. She likes to entertain at home and being with people. Quick to respond, forceful and competitive, she likes to win and has good leadership qualities. Hobbies would be travel (pronounced cheek bones) reading, specialty cooking, fund raising, remodeling homes (curved forehead). She loves to be by the water or in open spaces, and prefers rounded rather than geometric designs.

MICK JAGGER

Mick Jagger's protruding lips and length above the upper lip show he is a very impulsive person with a dry sense of humor. Here is a person who has the "gift of the gab". Does he ever stop talking? Mick is a very analytical person and pays close attention to detail. Notice the deep furrows between his eyebrows, he likes to get things exactly right. The inverted V-shaped eyebrow shows an appreciation of design such as in art, photography and architecture. The flat forehead implies he appreciates time on his own, which may be a challenge for him since he is constantly with people. At times he may prefer to read a book or escape to one of his favorite places. Because he is more administrative, he would prefer to oversee a project. At the same time he is very conscious of how much things cost, and he enjoys a bargain.

VANESSA REDGRAVE

Vanessa has extremely fine hair which suggests a person very sensitive to taste, touch, feelings and emotions. When her feelings are hurt, she may take a whole week to get over the incident. Her features are narrow, which shows she gains her confidence through knowledge. She may be intimidated when confronted by new and challenging situations. Vanessa has an appreciation of quality versus quantity, and she enjoys being in an elegant environment. The music needs to be softer because loud noises or people will irritate her. The thinner upper lip shows that she is a concise person, not interested in wordy discussions. She likes to come to the point quickly, but has the need to analyze situations or new products. Her sloping forehead shows a mind that works quickly, and she jumps to conclusions before all the information has been given. One eye appears higher than the other, suggesting she is less conventional in her approach. Her forehead is more rounded on her right side and the left side looks more squared off. This reflects a swing mood. One part of her is the maintainer and the other side likes to start new projects. The fine hair indicates she enjoys elegant dining and soft music.

WHOOPI GOLDBERG

Whoopi is a very impulsive person, which may have got her into trouble at times. The sloped back forehead shows she is quick to respond to situations, whether an emergency or ad-lib. Her high protruding cheek bones say she loves to have variety in her day, and does not enjoy repetitive situations. Her round nose shows she has a natural curiosity and enjoys being with people. She is an extremely tolerant person, but catch her at a bad time and she will be less tolerant (one eye is closer to the center of the nose). Her high forward balance shows she loves to have an audience. Her pointed chin suggests she handles pressure well. However, there is a stubborn side to her nature.

She enjoys her home and at times may have been accused of being a pack rat. The larger lower lip shows she enjoys giving and sharing with others. If you ask her for directions, do not expect a concise answer. She will give you all the options and what to notice on the way. This is shown by her large upper lip.

ANTHONY HOPKINS

Anthony's eyelids are completely exposed, suggesting he will want to know the bottom line. At times he may appear ruthless, because of his direct approach. However, his sensitivity, which is seen with his fine hair, will help to balance the previous trait. The straight outer edge of his ear shows he has a pioneering spirit and likes to start new projects, although his curved forehead suggests there is a little of the maintainer in him. Because he likes to look at the big picture and act on it, at times he will be perceived as a moving force. His high self-confidence says he enjoys a challenge and may become quickly bored if life becomes too ordinary. He enjoys and expects recognition and appreciates the strokes that come with it. Quality comes before quantity. Soft music and fine dining are a part of his preferred lifestyle. The V-shaped eyebrows show that he likes to design and co-ordinate projects. He has a high appreciation of architecture and design. He loves to read and gather information, as shown by his rounded nose and the flatness of his forehead.

If you follow your bliss,
you put yourself on a kind of track,
which has been there all the while waiting for you,
and the life that you ought to be living is the one you are living.

-Joseph Campbell

TRAITS IN ACTION

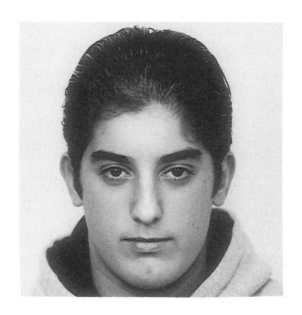

MARCUS

Eyebrows:	Appreciation of balance and harmony.
Hair (coarse):	Less sensitive to emotions and feelings. Enjoys the outdoors.
Thin upper lip:	Concise in his delivery of speech.
Nose:	Looks for a bargain, value for money.
Ear:	Likes to collect and enjoys investments. Has high music appreciation.
Forehead:	His rounded forehead indicates he enjoys his home and remodeling. He likes to maintain projects.
Width of face:	High self-confidence, enjoys a challenge.
Lower lip:	He enjoys giving of time and presents.
Careers:	Forest ranger, agriculture, investments, real estate broker, hotel management.

Hobbies: Wrestling, swimming, bicycling, bowling, tai chi, camping, concerts, art.

LINDSAY 7 year old twin

Ear lobes:	Enjoys collecting stuffed animals. Encourage her to have savings account.
High Self-Confidence:	Enjoys a challenge. Good leadership potential.
Eyes:	Very analytical. Strong need to know why.
Eyebrows:	The top of her eyebrow has a peak, this indicates design appreciation.
Iris:	Lindsay displays warmth and magnetism. Friends will tell her their problems.
Lower lip:	She has a big heart and enjoys giving of her time and presents.
Chin:	Lindsay does not like being pressured into an

activity. Give her the reasons why.

Career: Teacher, electronic engineer, writer occupational therapist, composer.

Hobbies: Poetry, have a collection, reading, writing, analytical games, singing.

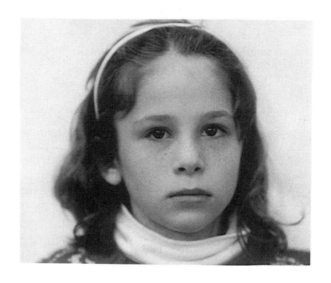

GINNY 7 year old twin

Eyes: She is an extremely tolerant person and tries to fit in too many projects. She likes the big picture. It is a challenge for her to stay focused. She has a need to analyze and ask questions.

Width of face: She enjoys a challenge. Very confident.

Ears: Has a love of music and enjoys having a collection. She likes to keep her possessions for a long time.

Thinking: Ginny is more sequential in her thought process. She needs to give herself plenty of time to study before tests.

Chin: Do not try to pressure Ginny into an activity. She works well under pressure.

Forehead: The small mounds on her forehead indicate high imagination. This is seen in both twins. Her rounded forehead indicates she likes to maintain.

Careers: Psychologist, social worker, electronic engineer, hotel management, personologist.

Hobbies: Writing, art, singing, photography, pets, soccer, analytical games, collections, reading.

The main difference between the twins is the forehead shape. This reflects the career differences. Lindsay likes to start new projects.

EVELINE

Cheek bone:	Adventurous, likes a variety in her day.
Nose:	The bulbous nose indicates she is a very curious person. She has a love of new information.
Forehead:	The squareness of forehead, indicates she enjoys starting new projects. Does not like to maintain them.
Lower Jaw:	She is extremely authoritative
Width of Face:	High self-confidence.
Eyes:	Very analytical and extremely tolerant.
Careers:	Architect, couturier, librarian, landscape architect.
Hobbies:	Hiking, gardening, reading, dancing, travel, collect books, philosophical interest.

ALAN

Above eyebrow: Pays attention to detail.

Lips: Concise, uses fewer words.

Chin: Enjoys verbal or physical confrontation. This can be used positively in panel debates or physical activity.

Eyes: He has a swing mood in tolerance. The right eye is closer to the bridge of nose.

Eye Lid: He wants to know the bottom line, rather than a lengthy analysis.

Fine Hair: He is a very sensitive person. Prefers quality rather than quality. Enjoys refinement in clothing and interior design.

Eyebrows: This is a very friendly person and enjoys working with people. Balance and harmony

Careers:

are important to him.
Hospital or college administration, hotel
management, real estate broker, trainer.

Hobbies:

Investments, art, photography, cooking, coin
remodeling homes, sculpture, stamp
collection, coins, books.

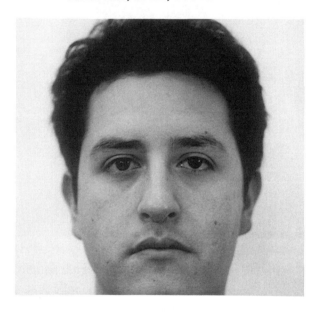

CARLOS

Eyebrows:

The inverted V shape eyebrow indicates
strong design ability. He appreciates balance
and harmony.

Hair:

He enjoys being in the outdoor and is less
sensitive to the cold climates.

Legs:

Because he has very short legs, he has a
physical need for exercise each day.

Nose: Carlos looks for a bargain. Enjoys investments. He   is somewhat skeptical, and will question new ideas until he can form his own opinion.

Chin: Works well under pressure and can be very stubborn.

Forehead: Quick to respond in emergency situations.

Careers: Engineer, stock broker, computer programmer, landscape architect, financing.

Hobbies: Music, jogging, dancing, soccer, photography, art.

DIANE

Forehead: Likes to maintain projects, remodel homes, enjoys cooking, work for an environmental cause.

Fine Hair:	She appreciates quality over quantity. Her feelings get hurt very quickly.
Jaw Line:	This is a very authoritative person.
Cheek bones:	Enjoys travel and likes a variety in her day.
Eyes:	Very expressive and emotional.
Lips:	Diane is very impetuous and likes to talk. She needs to think first before she speaks and acts.
Face:	There is more face in front of her ear, which indicates she enjoys being on stage.
Career:	Actress, radio or TV announcer, flight attendant, playwright.
Hobbies:	Hiking, tennis, theater, photography, travel.

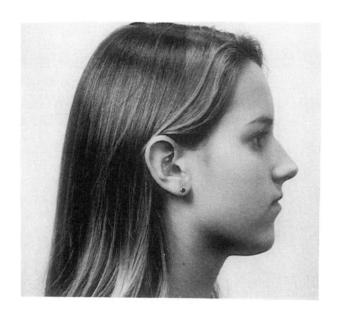

ALI

Sharp Face: She likes to ferret out information. Good for investigations.

Nose: Likes to oversee projects. The bottom line is how it costs.

Eyes: She has a swing mood on tolerance. Don't be late for an appointment with her. Although rhetoric cannot be seen in this photo, she places high importance on word usage.

Forehead: From the side view the forehead curves outward this indicates originality. Tie this in with her gift for words, she has the potential for writing.

Nose: Ali is very open to new ideas and is a good

	listener.
Ears:	Has a love of music.
Careers:	Hospital administration, writer, teacher, hotel receptionist, sales, accounting.
Hobbies:	Swimming, bicycling, horse back riding, cooking, writing, attend the theater and concerts.

TERESA

Eyes:	She is extremely tolerant and very analytical. She expresses warmth and emotion.
Eye brow:	Has a good sense of design and would make a great program director.
Width of face:	Teresa likes to take on new challenges and shows good leadership qualities.
Hair fine:	Because her hair is so fine, she will be very

	sensitive to other peoples' feelings.
Jaw Line:	She appears to be more authoritative and this will add to her leadership skills.
Lips:	Concise and to the point with out unnecessary verbiage.
Careers:	Lead workshops and seminars, training, computer programmer, occupational therapist, economist.
Hobbies:	Sing in choral group, art, photography.

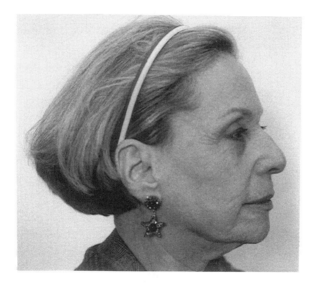

SUZANNE

Face Profile: She likes to plan long range, and is quick to respond to emergency situations. She may jump to conclusions or finish off a sentence for someone, because her mind works so

	quickly.
Lips:	Suzanne needs to think first, or she may commit to something or say what she regrets later.
Eye brow:	Very dramatic both in actions and speech.
Above the lip:	The length above the upper lip indicates she known for her dry wit.
Eyes:	Takes her work very seriously.
Nose:	Does not accept things at face value. Loves a bargain.
Cheek bones:	Needs to have a variety in her day.
Careers:	Television announcer, news commentator, sales, investments, artist.
Hobbies:	Tennis, gardening, reading, travel, theater, toastmaster, crafts.

APPLICATION TO LIFE'S DAILY EXPERIENCES

Personal Development and Awareness

A personology consultation is a non judgmental overview of an individual. It is a blueprint that allows one to look at each part of themselves objectively without feeling threatened. It gives insight into areas that may need a heightened consciousness in regard to positive or negative aspects of behavior.

People with a combination of high Self-Confidence, Authoritativeness and Objectiveness can be intimidating without intending to be. Each individual has a choice of modifying their behavior once they know their behavior is part of their genetic makeup. They can use these traits to their advantage. Recognizing the need to modify their perceived intimidation will help them to communicate with others who may score low in these traits.

Imagine a child whose traits are completely opposite to their parents' traits. This could present a problem and inhibit the child's personal growth and development. As some of you read this, I am sure you can relate to situations where you were neither encouraged nor supported in pursuing activities that interested you. There may have been times when you were struggling through school and your grades did not meet your parent's expectations. Worse still, you were considered to have a learning problem or you were considered not too bright. This situation could apply to any phase in a person's life if the environment, whether personal or business, is non supportive.

A recent newspaper article reported that a partition was placed around the desk of a disruptive child to isolate him from the rest of the class. His photograph showed him to be an extremely Tolerant (wide eye spacing) young man who was easily distracted. He had a multitude of ideas constantly going around in his head and had a very short attention span. If his legs were short and energy high, this would explain much of his tendency to be disruptive. Once these traits were identified both the teacher and the parents could handle the problem more constructively.

Personology allows us to take a good look at ourselves and understand others. It is not about answering a set of questions to decide which category you fall into, this study is different. Each person is as unique as their finger print. We are looking at our genetic structure that reflects our unique qualities and abilities. It puts us in touch with who we are and helps us to create a more balanced and harmonious life.

The Ten-Acre Principle

The ten-acre principle is an area that plays an important role in personal relationships and marriage. It defines the space around two people when they interact. Each person has their own ten-acre private domain. This domain should not be intruded upon by the other unless invited.

There is another ten acres which is shared by both sides. Individuals who are extremely considerate and ministrative are often accused of "butting in" to other peoples affairs when not invited. Their intention is to help others. This is often seen by others as interfering. It is best to ask others first before encroaching on their ten acres, no matter how much the individual appears to need help. In-laws are often guilty of invading the private ten-acres of their sons and daughters. For example, they visit their son and immediately take over. They change arrangements in the home or purchase items for the daughter-in-law without asking if she needs them. They may re-organize the cupboards or refrigerator. These actions step into the other person's ten acres and may cause bad feelings. In-laws should be there to play a supportive role and help out when asked.

Young children also need their own private area, whether it is their own room or a special place to keep their treasures. Children need to recognize their siblings private domain. This is often a problem as children move into their teenage years. Parents should insist that they respect each others privacy and space.

Marriage

An important ingredient for a successful marriage, or personal relationship, is understanding and respecting each individual. When two people are spending a good part of their lives together it is important to understand each other's traits and how they interact together. Do they clash or are they similar? Consider for example fine hair versus coarse hair. One person may prefer more elegance, softer music, quality rather than quantity and a more gentle approach to the relationship. The person with coarse hair may enjoy more of everything, whether it is sound, food, quantity versus quality or their approach to intimate situations. There may be greater differences, such as one person likes to be constantly active and on the go, while the other person enjoys just staying at home. When people have a combination of Analyticalness, high Self-Confidence, Critical Perception and coarse hair, they appear to put down or constantly find fault with other members of the family. This may not be their intent, just the traits in action. When people with these traits are aware of the negative communication they can consciously choose to override this tendency. Personology heightens the awareness of oneself and others, whether spouse, child or co-worker. It helps to eliminate misunderstanding and create a supportive environment.

Opposites usually attract each other. Before making the commitment of living together, couples should consider whether contrasting traits could cause problems. If so, can both parties come to an understanding of each other's needs and how to express them? Are there differences that each can live with? Each person in the marriage or relationship needs to work on their own traits and consider how to express their feelings in a positive way. It is not about "Well if he or she doesn't work on their traits then I won't." Each of us needs to set the example and be willing to grow in the relationship. Personology plays an important role in identifying each person's genetic traits and how they interact with one another. Following are some of the major traits that should be similar between two people in a relationship. Thickness of hair, tolerance, width of face, intellect and similar interest in people, information or things. Although this does not guarantee a life time relationship, it will certainly help the friendship be more compatible. Having a personology profile will help avoid conflicts and misunderstanding between spouses and family members. The profile helps to explain the differences and indicates the strengths and challenges. If you find yourself at odds with your significant other, look for what is good about the relationship and try to build on those qualities. A 1960 survey revealed that couples who had a personology consultation preserved their marriage in 88% of the cases.

Childhood Development

Knowledge of your children's traits significantly contributes to the understanding and handling of situations, whether communication or discipline. It helps in discovering their interests, level of physical activity and the types of sports or hobbies they enjoy.

A young boy who scored high on Acquisitiveness (enjoying collecting or investing) was asked what his hobbies were. It was not surprising to learn that he had a large rock collection that he had been collecting for many years. The parent who recognizes this trait in a child should encourage and support this type of activity. It's important to teach a child who has high Self-Confidence and coarse hair to be aware of others' needs. For the child who has low Self-Confidence be sure to acknowledge and encourage his achievements. When children have a sequential approach to learning, and are struggling with subjects they do not understand, be sure they understand each step of the learning process before advancing to the next level. Keep in mind this is the natural way of processing information for a sequential person. It does not indicate they are slow learners. Once this trait has been identified the student no longer feels frustrated. These students need plenty of time to study for their tests. Do not rush the sequential student.

Knowing your children's innate abilities and talents will assist a parent through the many stages of development. These include how your child communicates, how they feel emotionally and physically and how they process information. This approach to teaching is being used in private schools with great success. The children understand themselves and communicate with others better. Teachers are able to direct their students in constructive ways when their personology charts are available.

Business

Hiring the right person for the job makes all the difference in the world. How many people are truly happy in their jobs? A major problem in small restaurants is they often hire the wrong person for the job. The training is often insufficient and results in poor employee skills and customer service. Many times people move into management positions without adequate job descriptions, and lack good communication skills. The result is high turnover and unpleasant working conditions. This is always counter-productive. A boss who is highly critical, analytical, forceful, and has low tolerance would be very difficult to get along with. It is difficult to please this type of boss. Managers who are impatient can get very frustrated when a job does not move at the pace they demand. They seem intolerant when others do not live up to their standards or expectations. Once aware of their own traits they can choose to modify their approach and communicate more productively. A recent report indicated that the employees of a large sporting goods company had problems with two of the store managers. Apparently the employees did not receive training and thus were not suited to that position. This resulted in many people feeling very disgruntled.

Many companies use communication tools to improve corporate relationships. An example is one in which groups of employees observe each other's behavior and label those behaviors in select categories such as expressive-amiable, analytical-driver, etc. These communication tools help. However, with personology more information is obtained without verbal communication or group interaction in minutes.

Most accomplishments in business are the result of successful teams working together with diverse personalities and interests. Accurate and timely communication is crucially. Information must be communicated effectively. One of the biggest problems of communication is people receive information entirely differently from what was intended.

This is where personology plays a key role in business. Personology helps each person to develop a conscious awareness of themselves and those they interact with. This creates a higher level of communication and understanding which immediately raises the morale of the organization. Personology shows how and why people communicate and processes information. It shows the way they feel and respond emotionally to any given situation. It helps us to build an effective team.

Building an Effective Sales Team

No part of building a sales organization is more important than the selection of new recruits. "Personology was the significant contributor for developing a good team. Each recruit was given a copy of their personology chart with a detailed explanation of their strengths and weaknesses. This helped them utilize their strengths and add to their success in sales." - Don Wilson, CLU

Sales

Knowing your prospect within thirty seconds could make the difference between making the sale or not. Knowledge of your customer's traits will help you recognize the style of presentation and communication that will be most effective. In today's competitive market, we need as many tools as possible to be successful. After reading this book you will better understand how and why your customer acts or reacts in particular manner. For example when your client is more Discriminating be more formal and avoid using first names (unless this has already been established). Allow more time and space during the negotiations and do not press for a decision, particularly if they also score high on Automatic Resistance. If the client has high Self-Confidence and high Tolerance use larger gestures. Prove you know your subject well. Respond with assurance and give them the big picture. When dealing with people who are more Subjective understand their need to process new information step by step. Give them time to think their decision through. Do not jump ahead or hurry them. If you press them into making a decision they will probably leave without buying.

Impulsive individuals may tend to buy on spur of the moment, especially if they are objective. They are quick decision makers. Learn to recognize those individuals who have Low Analyticalness (exposed eyelid) and a thin upper lip. They will want you to be concise, to the point and deliver the bottom line.

Following is a profile of a hypothetical customer you are meeting for the first time: Fine hair, high in Conservation, Analytical, low Self-Confidence, Concise, Automatic Resistance, Administrative, Discrimination and Interest in Information (as shown by a flat forehead rather than rounded). This person is looking for a quality product/service that will serve more than one purpose. The price will be important and they will want to know that they are getting good value for their money. The customer will ask to see similar products. They will want to know the reliability of the product. They also will want to know what they are getting for the higher price. They will need a full explanation of the different features and their benefits. They are not familiar with the brand name and would wonder how easy it would be for them to use the product. Is there instructional information included in the package?. They need to be reassured. If this is not addressed they may avoid buying due to lack of confidence in the reliability and sincerity of the sales agent. A sale can also be lost if the customer feels pressured into buying. When they are shopping for a service take the time to ask what they are specifically looking for. Respond to them based on how this fits their traits.

There are many key traits to look for when working with prospective clients. Following are examples of some of the key traits.

If your prospect has fine hair talk about the quality of the product. Be aware of anything in the immediate environment that may cause a disturbance, such as noisy children or loud sounds. If you have coarse hair, lower your voice and speak softer and firmer.

If your prospect has sharp features, high detail concern and low tolerance, know that very little will escape their notice. Be sure to point out the quality of the product and encourage him/her to examine the product thoroughly. Make sure they have a detailed understanding of how the product or service will meet their needs.

When the prospect has administrative qualities, place emphasis on the cost and value. Know they are looking for a bargain. However, if they have fine hair, they will not sacrifice quality for quantity, whereas the ministrative person will place more importance on the comfort and what will serve his/her needs. They are more realistic about the cost and perceived value.

If your prospect has coarser hair and you have a finer texture, be more vigorous in your presentations. Adapt a more positive style and use bigger gestures.

For a more discriminating client be more formal and allow them more time and space during the presentation. Recognize their need to be more selective. If they also have fine hair, emphasize the quality and how the product compares with others.

If your prospect is more affable and you are discriminating, appear more casual. Adopt a friendly approach and treat them as a friend.

When your prospect has high tolerance, they may appear to be disinterested and become easily distracted. Ask them result oriented questions. If they are also impulsive be sure they are confident with their buying decision. This will avoid a change of mind once they have left the sales arena.

If your prospect is less tolerant, respond promptly to their questions and be on time. If you have high tolerance, stay focused on the topic at hand. Once a topic is completed you can introduce other unrelated issues.

When your prospect is more skeptical keep in mind they automatically question anything new. They don't accept things at face value. Present them with the facts up front. They need to understand and feel your claims for the product are irrefutable.

If your prospect has low analyticalness keep in mind they like direct action. They will be turned off by long drawn out sales presentation. Once they have grasped the concept move quickly to the buying decision. Understand they want results not a long drawn out discussion. This information will maximize your customer service best when one trait at a time is studied. Once you understand a specific trait and are able to use it in a one on one communication, introduce another trait. Once several traits have been introduced you can begin combining the traits. You will see how one trait will effect the other. Or, better still, take a sales workshop based on personology.

Jury Selection

There are many strong indicators in the face which reflect the way an individual will act or react. Personology will help by identifying these tendencies before the trial begins. In this way the attorney can better predict the favorable responses of those selected. They will then be able to direct the questioning and eye contact in a way that will support a positive outcome for the case.

Dr. Bruce Vaughan, a specialist in trial psychology, is considered to be among the foremost trial consultants in the country. He states that personology significantly contributed to the success of the cases won, 80%. In his jury determination he creates an ideal profile and a negative profile. This assists in creating a clear picture of the panel which will best serve your case and those you do not want on the jury. Once these profiles have been determined, personology will then help in selecting the people who best fit the ideal profile. It gives the attorney insight about jurors that would not otherwise be available. This insight can be used throughout the trial for directing or making eye contact with a juror. When the attorney wishes to emphasize a point an immediate reaction will be noticed.

There are certain people who will not help your case when representing the plaintiff.. When stress is indicated by the white of the eye being exposed under the iris, the person may be going through strong personal problems that would distract from the trial issues. Skeptical and Critical jurors are harder to convince, and might well cause a delay in the process or result in a hung jury. The following are some examples of traits which can be matched with the best-case and worst-case jury profiles.

The person with an Administrative nose is tight on money. If the case involves a dollar settlement, and there are several people on the jury with this trait, then an attorney would need to increase the sum to get a settlement closer to the acceptable compensation. In contrast a juror with a larger lower lip, indicating generosity, would be favorable to the plaintiff and would be inclined to award a larger sum.

Low Tolerance people like to live by the rules and it is doubtful that anything that is said will change their beliefs. In contrast, an Analytical person is concerned with facts and figures. They will need to have all the information in place before making a decision. Individuals with high emotionality would be ideal for cases that involved abuse. Typically the wide faced people will take on the leadership role. Individuals whose features are very pointed will tend to be very fussy, especially if combined with low tolerance, analytical and criticalness. Be aware of individuals whose face looks very different from one side to the other, they may be very changeable. The individuals with low analyticalness may well speed up the process. Time is of the essence, they understand and want action. Their idea is "let's cut through the red tape to get what ever needs to be accomplished".

"Deep within man dwell those slumbering powers;
powers that would astonish him,
that he never dreamed of possessing;
forces that would revolutionize his life if aroused
and put into action"

-Orison Swett Marden

The Key to Finding Your Life Purpose

Book shelves are currently filled with subjects on how to solve the on-going challenge of making career decisions. Many offer self evaluation tests. Others have included charts that are designed to help you through the maze of career choices. All of these approaches can be very helpful in defining a career in today's changing market needs.

Much of this career searching activity has been stimulated by the dramatic increase in the number of people facing change. With the constant downsizing and reorganization of companies, many people are considering other job possibilities. They are asking themselves what really motivates them, and what options do they have to instill greater job satisfaction.

How many college students actually know what their major will be? Most change their major five or more times, and only 30% of post graduate students stay with their original major. Although they may have gone through one of the testing programs, something still does not feel quite right. They find themselves in the dilemma of still not knowing which direction to take their career.

Such was the case of Karen who graduated from Stanford with a chemistry degree. On her first day in the job she knew this was the wrong decision. However, by that time she had invested a considerable amount of money and time. She felt she needed to stick with her career choice, at least until something else came about. Looking for an alternative approach to her dilemma, Karen decided to have her personology profile made. The profile confirmed she would be happier working as either a technical writer or journalist. After disclosing this information to her, she mentioned her minor degree was in technical writing. At the time of the initial analysis this was not known. So why did she not come to that conclusion by herself. She had already invested a considerable amount of money and time, and having made a mistake once, she was being more cautious the second time around. She was seeking confirmation from an independent source. Her comment was "if only I had known of this service earlier."

As mentioned earlier, personology yields similar results to multiple-choice testing such as Meyers Briggs, Strong Campbell and the Enneagram. Major differences between those systems and personology are there are no questions asked and there is no "type casting." No two profiles are exactly alike. For each career suggested, the percentage of matching traits are given. A personology consultation can reduce trial and error and establish information that will help find the career path best reflected in each person's innate abilities. The consultation often validates what has already been considered and gives "permission" to move forward. Mary, who had taken many of these tests, felt frustrated because the results told her she fell in the middle. Her personology profile showed that she was a very diverse person and had the ability to do well in several careers. Her chart confirmed much of what she had sensed and created a clear path for the direction she planned to pursue. John, who is an engineer, felt there was something missing in his life. He enjoyed his work, however like many engineers he was putting in long hours. At the end of the day he felt exhausted and did very little with his spare time. He was not using his creative talents and this caused a great deal of frustration. The profile helped him rediscover his love of photography and nature, something he had not done in years. It renewed his passion and created an outlet for his artistic expression, bringing a deep sense of satisfaction. One that had been missing for years.

Choosing a college major or a career is a large investment of time and money. This is true whether you are a new college student, re-entering the job market or looking for a career change. It makes sense to seek advice and confirmation on a career direction that best reflects one's innate abilities. After all we are going to spend many years working, why not avoid the trial and error? So many people are finding themselves imprisoned in jobs they really do not enjoy. Because the job offers security, there is a reluctance to consider other possibilities. Living a life of compromise has no lasting satisfaction. It may even create a negative environment that overflows into the home, affecting the lives of those around you. Women, for the most part, ask themselves that soul-searching question at an earlier age, whereas men seldom allow themselves the luxury of considering a change. When they are in a secure company position, financial demands cause them to tolerate the lack of satisfaction, rather than risk pursuing a new career which would bring them greater personal reward.

A situation that comes to mind is a salesman who, although successful at his job, was not a happy person. Something was throwing his life out of balance. As a result he sought alcohol to escape the frustration, to the point where it was affecting his job and his family life. A personology chart was recommended to help him understand what was happening in his life. He discovered he was in the wrong profession. The comment made by the personologist, who was unaware of the drinking problem, was that his present job was enough to send him to drink. This man changed his job and experienced a significant impact on his life. He discovered he was more suited to operating heavy road equipment even though he had a slender build. He took a job in a construction company, which he really enjoyed, and his desire for alcohol no longer was a problem.

Creating a life that expresses who you are will bring you greater satisfaction in all areas of your life. Think of the times you engaged in an activity that you really enjoyed. Those experiences are some of the key indicators that your body is designed for. What are some of the sports you like to play? Are you good at organizing events or volunteering. Do you like to work with your hands molding works of art or playing a musical instrument. Do you like to work with people or do you prefer to spend time by yourself. Are you a rock climber or are you more stimulated by a game of bridge. All of these answers are in the face. The face gives us clues for our life purpose. It doesn't mean that is all we can do, because we ultimately have a choice. Knowing that we would make a better sales person than an engineer does not lock an individual into that career. By all means try others. It is better to know that a position may not work out rather than go blindly into a job that does not match your innate abilities.

Personology gives an immediate insight of the student or client's strengths and challenges, without having to first go through the lengthy testing or interviewing. Many individuals have said the information gained from one personology consultation was equivalent to several sessions with a counselor, and uncovered the same information.

Having a profile made at the initial stages of working with the client, will offer the counselors and teachers another tool to identify traits which may explain some of the clients challenges. Such as, if the individual is more backward balanced, you will know immediately they have a tendency to hold on to their negative memories and associations. Churning them over and over in their mind like a broken record. If the client/student's face is very asymmetrical, you will be able to recognize they are subject to many mood swings and appear very unpredictable and inconsistent from one moment to the next.

The profile explains why some individuals lack self-motivation while others propel themselves at lightening speed through life. It explains why some people like to be by themselves and others are much more outgoing. Once the client is aware of these traits, they are able to deal with the situation more effectively. They can consciously chose to change direction in the moment.

Teachers will greatly benefit from this knowledge. They will be able to recognize the child's learning style and how to channel the child's natural abilities. The personology profile explains why one child takes on the leadership role, while another appears to be a loaner. They will understand why some children grasp new information so quickly, while others need time to assimilate the information, become confused or struggle to catch up. When a child is encouraged and supported by both parents and teachers to explore their own unique potential, the child will have a good foundation in place for making those all important college and career decisions.

Many teenagers have expressed their boredom in school and could not wait for the day when school was finished. If their area of interest had been identified at an earlier age, the school results may be very different. Such was the case of a teenager who spent one semester term taking a graphics design class. For him this was the best time in school. Unfortunately, the class was not offered again. The spark he gained from that one class went away and school for him resumed to the dull and boring routine again. It wasn't until he reached his early thirties, did he rediscover his natural talent for graphic design.

As parents, we all try to do the right thing for our children. When we understand what makes them so unique and different from each other, we are able to raise them in a supportive atmosphere. It is vitally important that we understand and recognize why Johnny is so good at soccer and Chris prefers swimming, why Karen loves gymnastics and Mary enjoys arts and crafts. When we are able to guide our children toward a life that gives them a great level of satisfaction, we are assisting them on their path to finding their life purpose.

Personology provides the keys to a lifestyle that will assist and support each individual on their path to finding their life purpose. When we understand ourselves, there will be a greater sense of balance and harmony throughout our lives. In turn personology will assist each individual to communicate on a more conscious level. Opening up a new level of understanding without passing judgment.

Creating a Map for Your Life

Now the journey begins. The first step is to take a look at your life and think of the times when you have engaged in activities that have brought you true enjoyment. Whether it was making puzzles, sketching designs, entertaining friends, cooking, being in charge of an event, sports, growing a garden or writing poetry. Write out a list of the natural skills you used when engaging in an activity or event that brought you a deep level of satisfaction. Ask yourself what brings the greatest passion deep down inside you? Now, cluster these skills together and notice if they describe a career that you would really enjoy. Let's take this one step further and define your innate skills based on your self assessment of your traits.

Following is a chart listing some of the traits which would influence career matches. Only the ones that have been described in the preceding chapters will be used. There are another fifty or more traits not listed in the book which are used to determine a career profile. These additional traits can only be assessed by a certified consultant.

The purpose of this exercise is to get a sense of how much of particular traits are developed in you. As you answer these questions, take a good look at your face in the mirror or get a second opinion.

This is just the initial step for creating your life purpose. In order to have a complete picture, contact the author for a consultant in your area.

Self-Assessment for Career and Personal Profile

This assessment will only create a limited career profile. In order to obtain the full range of careers that match your innate abilities, you would need to consult with a certified personologist, either in person or by mail. In order to find a consultant in your area, please contact the International Centre for Personology at the number given at the end of the book.

Foot Dexterity: The length of your legs compared to your torso - short, medium or long.

Hand Dexterity: The length of your three middle fingers - are they similar in length?

Risk Taker: Is your ring finger longer than your index finger?

Philosophical: With your palms facing you and your fingers together hold them up against a light. Can you see light coming in between them? Do not squeeze your fingers together.

Hair: Is your hair fine, medium or coarse?

Authoritative: Do you have a wide jaw?

Adventurous: Are your cheek bones very pronounced?

Takes Things Personally: Do you have a short upper lip?

Administrative: Does your nose have a hump (Roman Nose) on the bridge?

Ministrative: Does the bridge of your nose have a dip?

Self-Confidence: Is your face wide at the temples or narrow?

Tolerance: Are your eyes close together or are they further apart?

Sharpness: Do you have sharp pointed features?

Forward Balance: Is there more head in front of your ears or is it balanced?

Backward Balance: Is there more head behind the ear?

Physical Motive: Is the space between the base of the chin to the base of the nose short, medium or long?

Music Appreciation: Is your ear completely rounded?

Dramatic Appreciation: Do your eyebrows sweep upwards?

Esthetic Appreciation: Do your eyebrows form a straight line?

Acquisitive: Can you see the base of your ear lobes clearly when viewed from the front?

Objective/Subjective: Does your forehead slope back quickly or is it more vertical?

Construction: Do you like to start new projects?

Conservation: Do you prefer to maintain projects?

Analytical: Does the upper fold of your eyelid cover most of the lid?

Critical: Do you quickly see the flaws?

Rhetoric: Do you enjoy writing and have lots of ideas running around in your head?

Multiplicity of Ideas: Do you have lots of ideas running around in your head?

Imagination: Do you have a strong imagination?

Competitive: Do you enjoy competing with yourself or others?

Progressive: Are you action driven (C) or do you spend time thinking and not doing?(A)

Concentration: Are you able to concentrate for long periods of time?

Working with People: Do you enjoy working with people?

Working with Information: Do you like to work with information?

Working with Things: Do you like working alone with things and information?

Traits	Low=A	Medium=B	Much=C
Foot Dexterity:	_____	_____	_____
Hand Dexterity:	_____	_____	_____
Risk Taker:	_____	_____	_____
Philosophical:	_____	_____	_____
Hair:	_____	_____	_____
Authoritative:	_____	_____	_____
Adventurous:	_____	_____	_____
Takes Things Personally:	_____	_____	_____
Administrative:	_____	_____	_____
Ministrative:	_____	_____	_____
Self-Confidence:	_____	_____	_____
Tolerance:	_____	_____	_____
Sharpness:	_____	_____	_____
Forward Balance:	_____	_____	_____

Backward Balance: _____   _____   _____

Physical Motive: _____   _____   _____

Music Appreciation: _____   _____   _____

Dramatic   _____   _____   _____
Appreciation:

Esthetic   _____   _____   _____
Appreciation:

Acquisitive: _____   _____   _____

Objective/Subjective: _____   _____   _____

Construction: _____   _____   _____

Conservation: _____   _____   _____

Analytical: _____   _____   _____

Critical: _____   _____   _____

Rhetoric: _____   _____   _____

Multiplicity   _____   _____   _____
of Ideas:

Imagination: _____   _____   _____

Competitive: _____ _____ _____

Progressive: _____ _____ _____

Concentration: _____ _____ _____

**Working
with People:** _____ _____ _____

**Working
with Information:** _____ _____ _____

**Working
with Things:** _____ _____ _____

Once you have entered the results in the appropriate columns, take a piece of paper and draw two columns, marking one "A" and the other "C". From these columns cluster traits together to create a job description, for example.

If you have the following traits under the "C" column such as:
>information,
>concentration,
>design,
>organization,
>multiplicity of ideas,
>analytical and construction.

This cluster of traits would describe an electronic or design engineer, architect (general or landscape) reseacher or mechanic.

If you have the following traits under "C" column such as:
Conservation,
People and Information
High foot dexterity (short legs)
Objective
Affable
Adventurous
Ministrative
Acquisitive
This cluster would describe someone who is good in sales, work in a hotel or resturant. Health related careers such as nursing, Dietician, Dentist, Life insurrance, real estate.

If you have the following traits combining "A" and "C" columns:
Conservation,
Low tolerance,
People,
Information,
High foot dexterity,
Competitive,
Objective,
Rhetoric,
Ministrative,
Design,
Organization
This cluster would describe someone who would be good at teaching, interior design, facilities planner, organizer, personal coach or sales trainer. Add physicalness to this cluster and that would be a Physical education teacher or coach.

Now create your own clusters and see how they fit a job description. This exercise has nothing to do with education or experience.

Examples of Career Clusters

Radio/TV Announcer
* Works well with people and information.
* Enjoys recognition (forward balance).
* Is quick to respond (objective).
* Impulsive.
* Has a competitive drive.
* Enjoys the limelight.
* (Dramatic appreciation will add to their skill)
* Rhetoric.

Dentist
* Enjoys working with people and information.
* A good maintainer (conservation).
* Looks after their clients needs (ministrative).
* Has very high standards (idealistic).
* Works well with their hands.
* Very generous individuals (automatic giving).
* Focused on their work (low tolerance).

Dietician
* Interested in information.
* Enjoy helping their clients maintain good health.
* Very idealistic.
* High standards.
* They enjoy researching new products.
* Will analyze new products thoroughly before recommendation.
* They notice every little detail.
* They are very fussy (sharp) about hygene.
* They tend to have lower tolerance.

* They are very focused.

Photographer
* They have a high appreciation of design.
* They are good at co-ordinating projects (organization).
* High appreciation of the esthetics.
* They have good hand dexterity.
* High imagination (a multitude of ideas running around in their head).
* They work well with information
* (If they have the ability to write well, this would benifit their career).

Personology Consultant (face language)
* Works well with people and information.
* Enjoys analyzing and interpreting the charts.
* They have high concentration.
* Good at design and organization of information.
* They are intuitive and very creative (multiplicity of ideas).
* If they are high in conservation, they will be good at maintaining client relationhip.
* If they are high in construction, the emphasis will be on reseaching new information.

Accountant
* Notices every detail (sharp).
* Is very focused (low tolerance).
* Enjoys working with finances (administrative).
* They will analyse and investigate ways to improve the clients financial needs.
* Good at organizing ideas and high concentration.

* This career is more suited to the long legged individuals, because of the long hours spent at the desk.
* High conservation will assist them in developing long term client relationships.

Nursing
* They are very affable and work well with people.
* They enjoy nursing patients back to good health (conservation).
* They enjoy servicing people (ministrative).
* Insatiable curiosity about information (rounded end of nose).
* They are quick to react in emergencies (objective).
* They are good at organization.
* This career is more suited to individuals who are shorter legged.

CAREER AND PERSONALITY PROFILE BY MAIL

Are you searching for a career and unsure about the direction? If so, then take the next step and fill out the form below. The career profile has helped thousands of people find a career that gives them a deeper level of job satisfaction.

To order a profile by mail, please fill out the following information and send 3 close up photographs. One full face with forehead exposed and one of each side profile with ear fully exposed. Please tie hair back close to the head. Make sure the photograph is close up. The face should fill the lens with a small border. Also send 6 pieces of hair from each side of your head taken from just above the ear. Tape the hair on the card and mark left and right.

Please answer the following questions:

1. With your palms facing you, are your three middle fingers similar in length? _____

2. With your palms facing you, is your ring finger longer or shorter than index finger? _____

3. With your fingers together and palms toward you, can you see gaps between the fingers? _____

4. Are your legs short, medium or long in proportion to you body?

_____

5. Do you spend more time thinking rather than doing?

_____

6. Or are you more action driven? _____

7. Are you competitive? _____

8. Are you direct or tacful? _____

You will receive a chart and tape with a detailed explaination regarding your strengths and challenges and traits you need to work on. You will learn how to use your traits to build both business and personal relationships. You will also receive suggestions for careers, advocations and hobbies that reflect your innate abilities. The fee is $55.00 which includes shipping. Thirty five pounds for UK residents. Checks written in English currency are accepted. Or you may elect to pay by Visa/Mastercard.

Visa/Mastercard
number:_____Expiration
Date:_____
Name   on
card:_____

_____
Address:
_____City_____

_____
State/County_____Zip/postal
code_____
Make checks out to: Naomi R. Tickle, P.O. Box 4439, Mountain View, Ca 94024, USA or you may fax your information to 415-965-9839 E-mail Naomitickl@aol.com.

Consultations

Personology consultations, based on detailed face readings, are available throughout the United States and Europe. These consultations offer the client significantly more information than the scope of this book. The accuracy of the measurements are much more precise since personologists use standard procedures and special tools. In this book a facial feature is considered either significant or it is ignored. The personologist, after completing the measurements, will categorize a trait as high, average or low. After the results have been calculated from the measurements they are documented as a permanent record on a chart.

Another service generally included in a consultation is career matching. A computer is used to search for careers which best match the client's innate abilities and traits. This service has nothing to do with salaries, availability of jobs or the client's experience. The major benefit is that it's only based on innate abilities, and is therefore valuable when clarifying new career directions. In the initial 1960 survey on vocational recommendations, 96% of surveyed individuals who had personology charts completed were satisfied with their jobs.

Even when a client is not currently interested in a new career, the results are fascinating and explain the yearnings and fantasies of earlier years.

In addition to the fifty-two traits described in this book, there are over fifty more traits measured during a consultation. These other traits are key indicators for career matching.

The last benefit of a consultation, of course, is objectivity. No matter how skilled you become, at personology, it is hard to be objective about yourself. We try to be fair to ourselves, but usually we are somewhere between trying not to flatter ourselves and trying not to be too hard on ourselves. The personologist has neither motivation, and can therefore provide an unbiased perspective.

This service is highly recommended for high school and college students. Parents and students invest a large amount of time and money in education. A small investment will help avoid the frustration experienced by many of finding the right career. Why have a life of compromise when there is a system available which will assist you in making those all important career decisions.

GLOSSARY OF TERMS

ACQUISITIVENESS	The need to acquire possessions
ADVENTUROUSNESS	Inclination towards change and excitement
ADMINISTRATIVE	A natural tendency to administrate/oversee
AFFABLE	Enjoys meeting people. Very approachable
ANALYTICAL	How much a person analysis
AUTHORITATIVENESS	Naturally authoritative
AUTOMATIC GIVING	Automatic giving with no strings attached
BALANCE BACKWARD	Relates to what has happened in the past
BALANCE FORWARD	Think in terms of the future rather than historical
CONCISENESS	Brevity of expression
CONSERVATION	To maintain and look after
CONSERVATISM	A more conservative approach to high risk
CONSTRUCTION	Enjoys starting new projects, does not like to maintain

CREDULITY   To be open to new ideas

CRITICAL PERCEPTION   An awareness of variation from the rule

DETAIL CONCERN   The habitual focus on detail

DISCRIMINATIVE   To be selective

DRAMATIC APPRECIATION Exaggerated communication and action

DRY WIT   Dry sense of humor

ESTHETIC APPRECIATION An appreciation of balance and harmony

EXACTINGNESS   The need to have something exactly right

FOOT DEXTERITY   The need to sit or stand

GROWING TREND   Interest in all aspects of personal growth
                             and horticulture

HAND DEXTERITY   Coordination of the hands

IDEALIZING TREND   A conception how things should be.
                             Realistic or idealistic

IMPULSIVENESS   To respond instinctively both verbally
                             and physically

INNATE SELF CONFIDENCE Built in self confidence

JUDGMENT VARIATION   Unconventional approach

MENTAL MOTIVE   Amount of Mental activity

METHODICALNESS	The habitual reliance on methodical routine
MINISTRATIVE	To spontaneously serve and look after
MOOD SWINGS	To suddenly switch to a different mood without any warning
OBJECTIVE THINKING	The timing of the mental process
OPTIMISM	Habitual attitude of thinking positive
PHILOSOPHICAL TREND	Strong philosophical interests
PHYSICAL INSULATION	The insulation to external circumstances
PHYSICAL MAGNETISM	The amount of warmth in a persons eyes
PHYSICAL MOTIVE	A tendency to react physically
PHYSICALNESS	Physical stamina
PIONEER	To explore new concepts and new territory
PRIDE IN PERSONAL APPEARANCE	Takes things personally
RHETORIC	An appreciation of correct word usage
SERIOUS MINDEDNESS	Takes life too seriously
SHARPNESS	Extremely aware of what is happening
SOUND APPRECIATION	A high appreciation of music

TAKES CHANCES	Risk taker
TOLERANCE	Timing of emotional action to what is seen or sensed
VERBOSENESS	The need to embellish a conversation

INDEX

Administrativeness,   62
Acquisitiveness,   108
Adventurous,   53
Analytical,   121
Authoritative,   43
Automatic-Giving,   55
Automatic Resistance,   59

Balance,backward ,   91
Balance,forward,   91
Burtis, William,   7

Conciseness,   64
Conservation,   119
Construction,   119
Credulity,   69
Critical-Perception,   124

Detail Concern,   93
Discriminative,   103
Dramatic-Appreciation,   99
Dry Wit,   58

Emotional Expression,   100
Esthetic-Appreciation,   106
Exactingness,   85

Foot Dexterity,   19

Hand Dexterity,	23
Impulsiveness,	67
Jones, Edward Vincent,	2, 5, 7
Judgement Variation,	126
Mental-Motive,	95
Methodicalness,	88
Ministrative,	62
Mood Swings,	9
Objective Thinking,	115
Philosophical-Trend,	29
Physical Insulation ,	30
Physical Motive,	95
Physicalness,	37
Pioneering Trend,	51
Pride in Personal Appearance,	57
Rhetoric,	128
Self-Confidence,	10, 75
Self-Reliance	47
Self Reproach,	84
Serious-Mindedness,	36
Sharpness,	89
Skepticism	69
Sound Appreciation,	97
Tenacity,	48
Tolerance,	79

Verboseness,   64

Whiteside, Robert,   5, 7

APPENDIX

Classes, Workshops and Services

Individual Charts for Career Guidance:
Whether you're a college student, re-entering the work force or in a mid-life career change, personology charts will help to eliminate confusion and assist in making important career decisions.

Personal Development and Communication:
Many people have experienced the frustration of never understanding who they really are. They have experienced a lack of identity or validation growing up within the family structure or in their personal and business lives. Personology gives each person a unique insight of themselves and how they can create a sense of balance and harmony in all aspects of their lives.

Relationships:
A personology consultation clearly explains the strengths and challenges within a relationship. The profile gives each person a better understanding of each other and avoids unnecessary confrontation and hurt feelings. Many couples have reconsidered separation after having their charts made and have subsequently stayed together.

Seminars and Workshops:
Would you like to increase your sales, improve employee relationships and communications? We offer half and whole day workshops which are held on-site or at locations which are more relaxing.

Personology as a Profession:
Are you interested in becoming a Certified Personologist? Correspondence courses are available. Please contact us at the address below.

Profile by Mail:
Profile by mail includes a chart and a thirty minute tape with a detailed explanation of the following areas in your life; Careers, Advocations, Hobbies that reflect your innate abilities and your personal strengths and challenges and how they relate to relationships. Send three close up photographs (3x5 inches, full face and profiles of both sides (ear exposed) plus at least ten strands of hair (taped to a card) from each side just above the ear. Mark which side they come from. $49.00 per person. Checks, Mastercard/Visa are accepted.

Additional Copies:
Additional copies of *It's All in The Face* may be purchased directly from the address below.

Call or write to:
Naomi Tickle
Face Language International
723 Vanessa Way
Petaluma, CA 94952
Tel: (707) 769-0290
Fax: (707) 769-0342
e-mail: naomitickle@aol.com

About the Author

Naomi Tickle is a certified Personologist. She is the founder of the International Center for Personology and a world renowned face reading expert. Her interest in personology began fifteen years ago during her studies at the Academy of Color in San Francisco. Like many, her first reaction was one of skepticism, however curiosity got the better of her and she signed up for a Personology profile. Her profile was amazingly accurate and she felt for the first time someone really understood her.

During the next fifteen years, Naomi launched the Institute of Color and Design working with private clients and offering color training programs. During this time she noticed that color groups told much about people, such as their preference for antique or modern decor, geometric or flowing pattern apparel, and their preference for geographical environment. Her continued research with clients suggested a probable genetic link between color groups and innate preferences. Intrigued by these patterns Naomi devoted two years to the study of personology.

Naomi has taken her work, in relating physical characteristics to psychological characteristics, a step further in this treatise on personology. Naomi supports others, through her practice, on their quest for self-knowledge and finding their life purpose. Whether an individual is looking for the career that follows their heart's desire, or seeking a deeper understanding of themselves personology provides an approach to discovering a part of the human puzzle.